Kissing the World Goodbye

by
Jennifer Clark

Table of Contents

To my brother and sister

There is a Vietnamese proverb: *Brothers and sisters are as close as hands and feet.*

This sister couldn't ask for two better sets of hands and feet to help me make my way through this world.

A Fleeting History of Phylum, Class, Order, and Family

WHEN MY FATHER admits he's had blood in his urine for weeks, my mother yells at him. *Don't worry,* he says. *The storm will blow over.* Instead, she drags him and, as it turns out, his ratty, tatty bladder to the doctor.

Tiny stones have been sloshing in his bladder for months, tearing the delicate lining. He tells the doctor that a biopsy is not necessary. *I do not have cancer. Take out the stones if you wish, but no plucking of the bladder.*

Since when did you become a physician? my mother wants to know.

He's an engineer, isn't he? surmises the nurse.

No, he's a Ph.D., doctor of invertebrate zoology. Retired professor. Apparently, he knows everything.

Ph.D.s, the nurse sighs, *are the worst.*

In response, my father offers up a possible correlation between his current condition and the time he dangled from a tree when he was six.

*

When my father turns nine, over nine thousand miles away from his hometown of Belding, Michigan, men on another continent finish building a road. A fresh wound, it winds its way from the Tasmanian foothills of Hobart to the top of Mount Wellington. It is the Great Depression, and Albert Ogilvie, the premier of Tasmania, promotes the project, paving a way for thousands of unemployed Australians to work. Locals refer to the road as Ogilvie's Scar.

When my father is twenty-eight, he'll cross the Pacific Ocean and ride a motorbike up and down the Scar at least once a month for a little over a year.

Here, in Tasmania, he learns to read clouds. Wisps of white wrapping around the peak of the mountain means cold winds and miserable weather. He's been up there, four thousand feet above sea level, when snow blows horizontal and skins of ice lay on the mountain's many ponds. So, even though a handsome day hovers in Hobart—*lovely enough for a picnic*— and despite his desire to search for the Tasmanian isopod, he does not. He waits below.

*

On Mount Wellington, ferns grow the size of trees. Charles Darwin, in his book *The Voyage of the Beagle*, wrote:

In many parts the Eucalypti grew to a great size, and composed a noble forest. In some of the dampest ravines, tree-ferns flourished in an extraordinary manner; I saw one which must have been at least twenty feet high to the base of the fronds, and was in girth exactly six feet. The fronds forming the most elegant parasols, produced a gloomy shade, like that of the first hour of the night.

The Scar not yet carved in 1836, it took Darwin two tries to reach the top. *A severe day's work*, he noted. Having collected over a hundred species of insects, including the dung beetle, weevil, and bee, he got back on his ship, *the Beagle*, and sailed away.

Darwin didn't find the freshwater isopod, cousin to crabs and crayfish. Gilled creatures, these crustaceans are common marine, freshwater, and terrestrial animals with seven pairs of legs. *The one most familiar to you,* my father says, *is probably the one that rolls up in a ball when disturbed after you pick up your flower pot. But the Tasmanian isopod is part of an ancient group. Because it appears more flattened on the sides, rather than flattened from top to bottom, it folds not into the shape of a ball like our Michigan isopods do but into a disc.*

More like a Frisbee, I venture.

No, Frisbees are more uniform, my father corrects me.

How about a hockey puck?

Too smooth. Remember, the isopod is segmented.

A tiny, ruffled hockey puck?

Okay, that'll work. And then a minute later, *Maybe a donut since they can curl around a twig. Or a bagel,* he says, laughing. *Yes, a bagel is better.*

From his recliner, my father grows increasingly animated talking about isopods, more commonly known as pill bugs or roly-polies. Pressing his hands together with his palms outwards, he wiggles his fingers. *Imagine,* he says, *pairs of legs protruding from your stomach.* He goes on about evolution, exoskeletons, ligaments attached to muscles, and the *glorious mechanics of these humble creatures!* My mother rolls her eyes, shrugging him off as he tries to ride us up the mountain.

Even when you know what you are looking for, these animals aren't easy to find. Darwin probably stepped on one, though, my father says, surmising that the British naturalist most likely sloshed through the shallow pools where the diminutive crustaceans reside, their small brown bodies blending in with the sediment.

Dotting Wellington's many pools are mossy-looking steppingstones. *These inviting stones aren't stones at all*, my father explains, *but* Abrotanella fosteroides, *a hard, cushion-like plant.*

With practice and patience, you start to understand where the isopods will be. Pick up stones, debris, and strange sediments. Lift up a clump of grass. Find out what they prefer.

*

Crouching over a pond on the mountain, my father uses a kitchen strainer to scoop up sediment. He gently sifts; the smaller particles slip through the holes and back into the water. He then ladles the crustaceans, along with bits of debris, into a cake-sized, white enamel pan. The white allows him to identify and sort the tiny bodies more easily. He collects, counts, and measures. Up and down the mountain, month after month. Collecting, counting, measuring. He'll take pictures of preserved isopods after he positions their bodies precisely, smallest to largest, rows of brown commas on a page and no words between them.

*

On the eve of my father's surgery, the tulip tree in the backyard grows weary and releases one of its large limbs. As the ground shudders, my mother fears her world is slipping away.

*

This is a fact: My sister Holly and I are two continents. Ever evolving, we disassemble and collide. Just as we begin to drift away, we join together, only to pull apart in another area. Holly is always the helper when someone is in need. There is no give to her giving, and this creates tensions between us.

The other day she mentioned she was going to clean Cecilia's windows. *Who,* I wanted to know, *is Cecilia, and why are you cleaning her windows? And who will watch your baby?*

My comments grinded against Holly's good nature, and she scrunched up her face. *She's my eighty-eight-year-old grocery customer, and when she came through my line the other day, she told me she has dirty windows, okay? Who else is going to do it for her? And not that it's any of your business, but I'm bringing King with me. Cecilia will love to meet him.*

Holly now sets her sights on the tree limb lounging on our parents' lawn. Donning new work gloves and gripping a pristine chainsaw—the plastic sleeve still covering the chain—she bursts into their home and marches past their startled expressions and into the backyard.

When my sister calls, she is hysterical, sputtering about tulip trees and our *bitch* of a mother. *You know,* she weeps, *the apple doesn't fall far from the tree.*

Whoa, I say, trying to rein her in. *Just take a deep breath, little-miss-apple-who-has-also-fallen-from-the-tree-and-is-now-rolling-down-the-hill-at-deliriously-high-speeds.*

*

The morning of my father's surgery, I'm sitting in the hospital waiting room with my mother. *I've about had it with your sister and her phone calls,* she says. *And then she just shows up at the house, with a chainsaw no less. So here I am, screaming at your sister. I'm trying to keep your father calm the day before his surgery, and your sister didn't seem to understand that. I don't want you taking care of the tree, I told her. The last thing we need right now is you getting hurt. I don't want you doing it. She wouldn't listen. She asked if I wanted her to leave. Yes, I said. Leave and don't come back. So Holly and her chainsaw left.* My mother sighs. *I hope she'll show up today.*

She'll show up, I say. I can already feel her pull.

*

Alone on the summit, he crouches over the pond and hears only wind.

*

Holly breezes into the hospital waiting room, latte in hand. She embraces my mother and kisses me on the cheek. *Don't you just love my new purse?* she says, modeling it on her hip.

The red is fabulous, my mother agrees. The tree fight is now ancient history. Call it a keen aptitude for forgiveness or a defective short-term memory gene; our family is not one to hold grudges. It's one of our best qualities.

A nurse invites us into the pre-op room where my father, gowned in paper, is propped up on a bed. His feet, covered in puffy red socks, stick out at the end.

Honey, says my mother as she takes his hand, *what nice socks they gave you.*

That lets us know he is a fall-risk, says the nurse, checking the IV that pumps fluids into my father's vein.

12

Oh, my mother utters in a soft, surprised voice. She pats her husband's wrinkled hand. I don't think I've ever seen her do that before. That simple gesture makes me want to cry.

My father clears his throat. *I just want you to know that if, well, um … know that I've had a good life.*

For God's sake, Joe! erupts my mother, releasing his hand. *You've been saying that since the day I met you.*

*

I'm here because of silkworms, my father is fond of saying.

He was born near the Flat River, in a town once known as the Silk Capital of the World. Each year, one million pounds of raw silk from silkworms who feasted on mulberry leaves in Japan, China, and Italy, poured into the tiny town of Belding, Michigan.

A silkworm is really a caterpillar that emerges from the blind, flightless moth *Bombyx mori,* which is Latin for silkworm of the mulberry tree. Domesticated and bred over five thousand years, silkworms produce fine fibers as they spin their cocoons. It takes one hundred and ten cocoons to make a silk tie.

*

Before she was a wife and mother, my grandmother, Julia Schmitt, was a Belding Silk Mill Girl, one of four thousand, mostly female employees of the Belding brothers, Alvah and Hiram. The Beldings built the first of four factories in 1886 and paid their employees well, some made as much as sixteen dollars a week. In walking distance of the mills, they built three more buildings called Clubs in which the girls, many of them recruited from farms far beyond the town, could feel at home.

In 1914, Bruce Calvert, an advertising writer hired by the Belding Brothers, wrote:

In these Clubs the girls have every comfort and convenience of the ordinary good hotel, much superior really to the dormitory service in high class colleges. Cozy, comfortable rooms, hot and cold water, plenty of bath rooms, lavatories with latest sanitary appliances, laundry, playgrounds, reception and reading rooms, music rooms, sewing rooms supplied with machines and cutting boards, and three good meals a day, all for $2.50 a week!

Julia lived in one of these Clubs and worked one of the Beldings' five hundred looms. Using silk strands that had been paired, twisted, spun, dyed, and wound onto bobbins, she created silk cloths used for lining petticoats, suits, cloaks, and dresses.

One day, while walking home from the silk mill, Julia and her long, satiny hair caught my grandfather's eye. He also worked in the mills for a time, repairing looms and other equipment. Eventually, he wooed her away from what the advertisements called *the silks with happiness woven into them.*

But World War I shook the silk road, and, as silk unraveled from fashion, my father was born in Belding. As Julia did with all four of her children, she spun her youngest son at home. In 1928, Joseph Engemann spilled onto a brass bed and into a town of dyers, winders, spoolers, and weavers. Belding's last silk mill closed in 1932.

*

Twenty years before the Belding Brothers first began peddling silk threads door-to-door, a woman a world away—known as Miss Wandly—climbs Mount Wellington to get a better view of where her fiancé drowned in the Tasmanian river, the Derwent. With a hard stone of grief lodged in her throat, she watches the water sweep its way to the Tasman Sea.

A merry band of climbers soon follow in Miss Wandly's wake. When they reach the cliff of dolerite columns known as the Organ Pipes, the party, using white lead paint, smears their names in large letters on the throat of the mountain. But even as her grand cords bleed white, the mountain still sings.

*

After numerous treks up and down the mountain, my father flies back over the ocean to Belding, just in time for his sister's wedding. Not long after, near the summit, two towers pierce the mountain's skin so Tasmanians can watch TV

*

Some people grow old. Others disappear. They climb summits, never to return. Old towers are replaced with newer ones. Factories fold. Silkworms keep spinning.

*

Enrico! Holly bellows, waving her arms in the air as if she is trying to catch the attention of someone a mile away instead of on the other side of our father's bed.

My sister must look far away as well for he shouts back, *Holly!*

Enrico then introduces Holly to the blue-scrubbed urologist at his side and explains that Holly's the *best ever* grocery cashier. She also taught his kids fifteen years ago. I watch my father watching them as they lob conversation across his prone body.

You've got to be shitting me. Although that sounds like something my sister would say, I think it's Enrico. *I'm still waiting on that raspberry beer recipe you promised me,* he says, chuckling.

I'll write it down for you. Dad, do you have any paper?

Why don't you try his gown? I suggest.

Hmpf, Holly responds.

Is Joe your dad? Enrico asks incredulously, *because I'm his anesthesiologist.*

I want so badly to say, *No, she's just here to take his grocery order,* but I just glare instead.

Yes, Joe is my dad, and this, she nods her head toward me, *is his* oldest *daughter, Jennifer.*

I can't take another second of this frivolous banter. *This is all really lovely having an opportunity to watch you two catch up, but can we focus on the patient, the reason we are all here?* I point to my father just in case there is any question as to whom I'm referring to. This brings the anesthesiologist to his senses. My sister, however, narrows her eyes and glares at me.

We'll take real good care of you, Professor, promises Enrico in a reassuring, doctorly tone. The urologist—I forgot he was in the room—informs us that the surgery will last about an hour and then he'll update us. My mother, sister, and I nod in unison.

As my father is rolled down the hallway, a mist descends. The last thing I see is his billowy, white hair drifting away.

*

When mist deepens and visibility is reduced to one thousand meters, mist officially becomes fog. Nearby bodies can influence fog, a low-lying cloud.

*

In the waiting room, we can't see past the clock on the wall. The minutes tick by. My mother flips through magazines, and my sister looks at her phone. I drink coffee and slip away into my favorite childhood memory.

I am maybe six. I'm jumping rope on the sidewalk when my father, his lanky frame squatting in the middle of our driveway, calls me to his side. I squat down and, like him, fold arms across bent knees.

Isopod is all I remember him saying.

Heads bowed, we watch a miniature armadillo, half the size of a macaroni noodle, sail ever so slowly across a sea of stones.

No need to travel far to fall into the mysteries of the world. One only has to crouch down and pay attention.

*

Harvest fog when necessary.

*

California redwoods can absorb more than half their needed moisture by feeding on fog. In dry deserts, invertebrates, like isopods, ants, and beetles, may feast on fog. The Namib Desert Beetle welcomes fog by walking to the top of a dune and positioning itself along the sandy ridge; its very body customized for collecting misted breath.

*

Over forty million years ago, the Australian ark, anchored to Antarctica, broke away and drifted north. As the sea rose, the Bass Strait formed, separating the southern stern known as Tasmania. When this occurred some ten thousand years ago, the island of Tasmania and every living thing on deck was cut off from the mainland.

We adapt to our circumstances. We continue to drift.

*

The lifespan of an isopod is three years. Female Michigan and Tasmanian isopods both build baskets beneath their bodies, between their first several pairs of legs, and lay their eggs in them. The Tasmanian isopod's eggs are twice as big and their shells twice as thick as those of the Michigan isopod. Michigan isopods hatch two generations per year whereas Tasmanian isopods take three years to complete one generation.

Learning this, my father says, *I became sensitive to the causes of long generation time. Something that has followed me long after studying isopods.*

Isopods eat decaying plant and animal remains. In Michigan, deciduous trees shed each year, their leaves tumbling into streams and ponds.

I concluded, my father continues, *that the rapid input of nutrients enabled Michigan isopods to specialize for rapid life cycle, with quick growth and the ability to produce many eggs to capitalize on the period of abundant food.*

*

Here is an evolutionary secret: No matter what basket we've rolled out of, Belding rings within each of us.

Hold up your right hand with your palm facing you. Let your eyes travel from the base of the ring finger down the palm. Cross the heart line and come to rest in the confluence of the head and fate lines.

You are here.

*

On the Australian mainland, my father walks through the cloud forest of the Otway Ranges.

He kneels and digs into the dirt with a trowel. *I had to be careful to keep my distance from the abundant fern fronds, many of which had terrestrial leeches perched on their tips, ready to attach for a meal of my blood.*

Teeming throughout the forest floor are isopods the size of a pinkie finger, the largest terrestrial ones he's ever seen. A relative of the Tasmanian isopod, the *Phreatoicopsis terricola,* with its big body and rudimentary eyes, has adapted to a dim and moist life in shallow tunnels beneath the ferns and eucalyptus trees.

The transparent body revealed a gut full of what I assumed was organic rich soil. I put some in a jar without much water but adequate airspace, and they survived the trip back to Tasmania.

*

Everything is connected to everything else. My father taught me that.

*

Ancient waters run beneath our feet.

Below one-fifth of Australia is the Great Artesian Basin. Described as a water tank, a giant geological sponge, and a finite resource, it bubbles its way up through natural springs. The Australian poet Andrew Barton "Banjo" Paterson celebrated this water. In his 1892 ballad "A Bushman's Song," he wrote: *Till I drink artesian water from a thousand feet below.* In a later poem, "Song of the Artesian Water," he wrote of drought and men mining for water *[f]rom the silent hidden places where old earth holds her treasure ... As the drill is plugging downward at a thousand feet of level / If the Lord won't send us water, oh, we'll get it from the devil ...*

We, like Paterson, praise water. We also waltz it away. We drill, bore, and siphon away the largest supply of fresh water in the world; as it is depleted, groundwater drops, and the springs it feeds dry up. As we lose what is below, we lose what lives above.

*

Crimes against crustaceans tend to go unnoticed. Today, the once plentiful *Phreatoicopsis terricola* is endangered. Unless these isopods promptly learn to fly, they are tunneling toward extinction.

*

We are in the post-op room. My mother rests in a chair; the urologist, Holly, and I sit on the couch, my sister in the middle. The urologist tells us that, combined, the stones removed from my father's bladder are the size of a plum. To demonstrate, he presses his thumbs together and overlaps his forefingers.

The size of a grapefruit! Holly exclaims.

No, more the size of a plum, the urologist corrects.

An orange, she counters.

A juicy, purple plum, I say between gritted teeth, kneading her in the ribs. She pokes back, but for the moment settles.

The doctor seems impressed with the size of our father's prostate. He tells us that men his age tend to have enlarged prostates, but his is especially large, protruding into the bladder. He had to use a special instrument to lift it so he could sweep some stones that had lodged underneath it. With other men, he would simply have shaved the prostate down a bit, but with our father's funky—he threw out *funky* as if it were a medical term—blood disorder, he couldn't risk it. Medication will be given to shrink the gland over time.

Two times I tell my sister to shut up. She loves to ask questions. She has a habit of ladling question upon question without waiting for the answer, the answer not as important as the asking. *Shut up*, I tell her. I want to hear what the doctor is saying.

The tip of his penis will be a little sore.

My sister and I cringe. We don't want to consider our father's penis, let alone know that it will be sore.

*

In the recovery room, we want him to feel at home. We flurry about, encircling him. My mother moistens his forehead with kisses. *How is it,* I wonder, *that one of the grandest men I've ever known seems so small?*

*

Mountains are ever evolving, shaped by wind, rain, and ice. Gravity and time bear down upon mountains and towns, always bearing down.

Convicts once mined Mount Wellington for ice.

We take what we can from hardness.

*

In Belding, children ran down Liberty Street, begging the iceman for *a slip of ice,* his truck bearing frozen blocks of water harvested in winter from lakes and ponds. *On warm days,* my father said, *ice chips tasted so good.*

*

Bundled in memory, the shiny skeins of ice and milk and egg men unravel.

*

Did you survive each other? my father wants to know. We all laugh.

Despite being tethered to earth by a catheter, my father rises into the clouds. *I should be able to take care of that limb in the next day or so,* he muses, his voice far away.

My sister whips out her phone and proceeds to slash her forefinger wildly about like a conductor in the throes of a grand finale. *The tree is taken care of,* she announces, throwing her hands into the air. *I asked Gary to come out this morning, and he just finished. It took him three hours.*

Wonderful, my mother says, beaming at Holly.

I could have taken care of that tree myself, my father murmurs.

Holly's Raspberry Beer Cocktail

Yields 6

This recipe appears as Holly emailed it to me. She said she got it from *Southern Living*. The magazine has uploaded the recipe onto YouTube, which you can watch here: *www.youtube.com/watch?v=jTP3CvA7dkk*. Warning: It will make you thirsty.

— ¾ cup frozen or fresh raspberries
— 3 ½ (12 ounce) bottles of beer,* chilled
— 1 (12 ounce) frozen raspberry lemonade concentrate, thawed
— ½ cup vodka

1. Stir the lemonade concentrate and vodka together. This mixture can chill up to 3 days.
2. If you can't find raspberry lemonade, just use ½ container lemonade concentrate and ½ raspberry apple concentrate (or your flavor of choice).
3. Stir in the raspberries and beer just before serving.
4. Serve over ice.

*I also just use three beers. I mean, seriously. WTF?

Apology to the Grayling

WHEN THE MICHIGAN Department of Conservation declared that *our native grayling has followed the passenger pigeon and the heath hen into Limbo*, half of me was in the Northern woods of Manistee, slumbering in the ovarian cave of a one-year-old child.

Grayling and grayling never to come, I apologize for us. I am a descendant of we the people who killed the goose who laid the golden egg. I am sorry you looked so fine, swam so strong, and tasted so delicious.

Perhaps if you could have laid low and been less tempting of a beauty both inside and out, things might have turned out differently. I am not casting blame. I am not. I only want you to understand that when we cast nets with meshes smaller than laws allowed and caught you before you had a chance to spawn, we did not realize that the rainbow and brook trout we placed in your home would nibble your children to death.

Forgive too my ignorance, not knowing the story of you and the genocide of your kind by my people's hands. One set of those hands belonged to my mother's mother's father. He was just trying to make a living. He was a hard-drinking Irish logger who joined others and slew the leafy soldiers who kept your waters cool. Slaughtered in their forest homes, a spring harvest of trees unleashed sediments as their giant bodies tumbled to their deaths. Your delicate grayling eggs were buried alive. Generations and generations not to come, suffocated under murky blankets.

All this apologizing and I have left the waiting room. I am somehow here, in the early 1800s, under the canopy of achingly tall trees with bellies big from three hundred years of being. Into a stream hugged by juicy grasses, fish fall from the heavens. Grayling, sleek and graceful, fly underwater. Thousands upon thousands shimmer and glide. Shimmer and glide. One stops and raises his head. His mouth doesn't move, but he is talking all the same.

I am king of this river, he says. Shimmer and glide.

I have to laugh. To think that a fish believes he is a king.

It is true, the trees whisper.

Drink, says the grayling. Shimmer and glide.

Hands cupped, I dip into his river offering. Fresh as first snowfall, the water is so pure that it burns. It is too much to take in.

I return to this waiting room, a world emptied of a king's existence. An old woman in a salmon-colored sweater waits. Her saggy lids close and open over milky eyes.

Looking for an anchor to keep me from drifting back again into the 1800s, I plunge my hands into a stack of magazines. My fingers hook onto *Field & Stream*, the August 2008 edition. Smiling men in various poses hold huge fish. Page twenty and twenty-one is a centerfold, titled "The Beautiful and the Dammed." Splashed across its pages is an underwater picture of an obscenely beautiful fish. The coral belly glistens; speckles of black grace its tail and back. Unlike the men, the fish is not smiling. Its mouth droops as if anticipating its own demise.

Montana's state fish, warns the magazine, *a native trout, is becoming rare due to mining pollution.*

I want to grab the salmon-sweatered woman before she floats away and shout, *Don't you see what is happening here?* But grayling, I just wait. Wait like I did seventy years ago when only half of me was here. This time, though, I am snared in one of your trees. I did not realize some of its branches had latched onto my mind, and I have brought the last of you through time with me. Tired of remembering, the tree releases its offerings like swollen fruit into my hair.

Right here in this waiting room, where salmon woman now deeply sleeps, a mass of unborn eggs begins to hatch. Your brothers, sisters, and a cousin once or twice removed are tangled up in this ridiculous, rather embarrassing gelatinous fishy hairdo. My fingers comb through knotted, grayled-up hair. Fish fall out and flop at my feet. One sails across the room, smacks the beige wall with its wet tail, and slides down, dangerously close to the woman who has forgotten she is waiting for her name to be called. And you, grayling, land on my lap. There is only one thing to do. I swallow you whole and lick your iridescence from my lips.

Old friend, I shall never again see the likes of you. You have become a constant, nagging pressure—my left side to be exact—for you have slipped from your watery life and journeyed into the rough, barky soul of a tree that, weighed down by all that it has borne, has shed you into me.

I apologize if your new accommodations are a bit tight, but at least it is—a place.

I feel your scaly body press against my ribs, your tail flicks in anticipation against my spine; an eye peers out from behind my left kidney.

My dear grayling, the doctors won't find you. Just keep hiding. This world, which was not kind to you, is still not ready for such beauty.

Unapologetic Blackened Salmon with Lentils

Serves 4

This is my son's favorite fish dish.

— *1 cup dried lentils (red, yellow, orange, or green)*
— *15 ounces low-sodium chicken or vegetable broth (or 2 cups water)*
— *1 tablespoon harissa paste*
— *2 tablespoons butter*
— *1 salmon fillet (2 pounds)*
— *Blackened seasoning*

1. Sort and rinse lentils. (I love using the red ones since they look pretty with salmon. However, they tend to get mushy. We're fine with mushy, but if you're not, go with green lentils.) Put lentils in a pan with the broth, bring to a rapid simmer, and then reduce heat. Cover and simmer gently for about 20 minutes. Within the last minute or two, stir in the harissa paste. (I use Trader Joe's Traditional Tunisian Harissa Hot Chili Pepper Paste.)
2. While the lentils simmer, make blackened seasoning. Set aside.

3. Remove skin from the salmon. (If you have never done this or haven't done it well in the past, watch this video, in which Jamie Oliver teaches you how to skin a salmon fillet in under 5 minutes: www.youtube.com/watch?v=9zI6uUqvvPE.)

4. Warm a large, heavy skillet on the stove.

5. Sprinkle half of the mixture over the skinned side of the salmon. Lightly rub in spices. Toss half the butter into the skillet and place salmon (seasoned side down) in pan. Immediately season the other side. After 5 minutes, toss remaining butter into skillet and gently flip the salmon, cooking it for an additional 5 minutes.

    Note: Depending on the thickness of salmon, time may vary from 2-7 minutes per side. Serve with lentils.

For blackened seasoning, mix together:
— *1 tablespoon Cajun seasoning*
— *1 tablespoon paprika*
— *1 tablespoon Old Bay seasoning*
— *2 tablespoons lemon pepper*
— *1 ½ teaspoons cayenne pepper*

Measured Thoughts on Cooking (in no particular order)

THREE STATES BREATHE between us, so my sister and I only witness our brother's doings on family vacations, like this past summer at the beach house in Wrightsville Beach, North Carolina. The large, two-story clapboard home has been in his wife's family for years, and for the past decade it has weathered our family gatherings. Here, North and South meet. The gravitational forces that pull us together are almost visible.

*

We surge into the house, and for one week our familial bodies—six big ones and five of lesser mass—orbit each other. The paths we take, while far from worn, are familiar. We rise and fight and laugh and drink. We build sandcastles and then knock them down. We toss wet swimsuits on the line strung along the back porch. On the front porch we rock in chairs and watch the comings and goings of the world. We read books, flip through magazines, and nap. Most of all, because we are in the vicinity of my brother's cooking, we hum around with the same fine food in our bellies.

*

For much of our time together, my brother pens himself up in the kitchen where he is like a bull on steroids. He stampedes about, yanking down spices, opening and shutting the oven door, and rushing out the back door to step out onto the porch to check on the grill. Right now, he is calm. His hands gently pat a dry rub over a tender filet of beef. Then, without warning, his nostrils flare. He charges over to the refrigerator and yanks out a freezer bag filled with chunks of freshly frozen pineapple.

*

He blends relentlessly. The cacophony of frozen fruit and coconut milk is deafening. Currents of loose conversations are churned up in his doing.

*

My brother hands out frosty glasses. I am not a coconut fan, but, because John made it, I accept his offering. The piña coladas are delicious.

*

I was watching the Food Network, and this chef—I forget her name now—had her face mere inches from the tripe dish she was preparing. She could have reached out and licked it with her tongue if she wanted to. My brother and sister are intimate like that when it comes to food.

*

I catch my brother inspecting the chicken with aromatic spices pinched between his fingers. He draws his hand back, high above his head, then hurls it down, lashing the meat with fresh rosemary. I keep my distance.

*

At the beach house, we eat and drink like kings.

*

Blackened salmon. Habanera margaritas.

*

John measures out guava nectar and pours it into the blender. My sister, Holly, slices a lime and tells him how she adores guava nectar too.

On the surface, my brother and sister appear much alike. They both care for people through food. There is no cup big enough to contain their generosity. As John adds a dash more of guava nectar, it occurs to me that I am more measured in the way I love.

*

Shrimp scampi. Chilled asparagus. Tomato bisque soup.

*

I remember my mother hadn't been feeling well, and I took over some homemade pea soup.

Pea soup, she sighs, *is my favorite.*

I know, mother. You've told me a hundred times.

She plows on as if I haven't spoken. *Yet, because your father thinks he's allergic to peas, I haven't been able to serve it for over forty years.* Over soup, she says, *of my three children, you are the hardest to know. I often wonder what you're thinking.*

I think but do not say, *To know someone, pay attention to what they do.*

*

I wash dishes and wonder if this comparison holds true for all people: that we cook like we love? I want to love better. The blender whirs, catching these thready thoughts and turning them ragged. I seize the neck of a carafe—slick with vinaigrette tears—and thrust it below the sudsy water. A hollow sob slips from its oily body.

*

Bodies, browned by the sun, fill the front porch. We rock in weathered white chairs; their tall backs draped with beach towels snap at the humid air. Two of us dangle our legs from the porch swing. Some of us stand. One of us eases into the hammock. Blackberry smoothies twirl on our tongues.

The ocean waves ceaselessly. From a rusted ceiling hook, a plastic plant sways in the salty air. Muddy leaves flutter against a blue, unflappable sky.

*

My brother is deep like the ocean. On the surface, waves of funniness knock you down. If you aren't careful, you can get caught in the seaward pull of his humor, which, from years of practice, streams long and shiny out toward the horizon.

*

When John isn't cooking, he practices medicine. Reach his side and you may find that still, quiet place in which a boy decides to become a doctor. *Which kind of doctor do you think helps the most?* he will ask.

Or, depending on the day, flounder into the deep doubt of infectious disease. Here, in these infested waters, people are drowning everywhere. Even when someone can be saved, there is not always land in sight on which they can safely be laid down. *How much help am I really,* he will ask, *when my patient is forced to choose between dying or having an infected body part removed because he can't afford the necessary medication?*

*

My brother carries the lost and wounded with him.

*

Face glossed in sweat, he stands before the grill, gently prodding stuffed zucchinis with silver tongs.

*

Somewhere, an artist who sculpts with his hands for a living chooses to have a finger cut off.

*

A mounting tidal wave of pots and pans threatens to envelop the kitchen.

*

My brother grows weary. I worry he will be dragged down by the weight of it all.

*

I find that the more helpful I try to be, the more I get in the way. Sometimes, swimming away is the best option.

*

Cooking shall save him, I think, just as a wave of Calphalonian magnitude crashes to the floor. Holly rushes to help.

*

My sister is a food emergency responder. The Queen of Substitutions, Holly is better than any cookbook or online culinary reference out there. She's saved countless dishes for me. When I call to inquire if I can substitute something for something else—say milk for heavy whipping cream—I have to put up with admonishments like, *What the hell are you thinking?* or *Do you really want to kill your family?* But it's worth it as she always comes through for me. Ultimately, she'll ask a series of rapid-fire questions and then pronounce what I should do. I pretty much follow her advice.

*

Hey, Hol. I get right to the point as there is no time to waste. My guests are arriving within the hour. *I'm making a chocolate peanut butter cheesecake, and it calls for a ganache on top. I don't have the exact ingredients, and I was wondering if I could substitute—*

Ganache, she interrupts.

What?

Ganache. You pronounced it more like ganoshe, and it's ganache.

Well, either way, can I—

Just tell me the ingredients.

I run through the list, and she barks out, *Don't do it!*

Do what?

Make the ganache.

Why not?

You didn't get the right kind of chocolate for it.

But it looks really pretty on the picture. All shiny.

Does the top of your cake look good? Does it have any cracks?

No, I reply.

No, what? That it doesn't look good or it doesn't have cracks?

It doesn't have any cracks.

Then don't do it.

I won't.

You'll ruin it if you do it. Don't.

I said I won't. I can tell from the way she's holding her breath on the other end of the phone that she doesn't believe me. But I am telling the truth this time.

I don't make the ganache, and Holly, as usual, is right in her cooking advice. The dessert, with its heavy cream, peanut butter, dense cheese, and dark chocolate, oozed with richness. An extra layer of chocolate would have made the cheesecake unbearably sweet.

*

But even the Queen of Substitutions and knower of all culinary questions and pronunciations accepts the humble role of sous-chef around our brother. She, like me, tries not to get in his way. As he swirls around us, she'll stand at the counter, dicing onions or chopping celery. I'll hunch over the sink, washing or drying a bowl while attempting to be a well-placed, non-descript shell on the shore of this churning, siblionic sea.

She'll cover a dish in aluminum. I'll lower my dishtowel. We step aside. We part and let him pass. We bow low. Our brother crests between us, reaches for a shelf, and pulls down cumin or salt. Swept up in these siblionic movements, there is a reassuring ebb and flow to what we do.

*

Sibilant is a real word. An adjective. It describes consonants that are pronounced with a hissing sound. Like the word *sister* or the sound of pleasure. *Siblionic* is a term I made up. It means a tangle of one.

*

Ever since we were little, people have had difficulty telling my sister and me apart. *Are they twins?* strangers would ask in grocery stores, banks, and parks. And my mother, having been asked this enough, came up with a response she was quite pleased with. *Why, yes. They are.* She'd wait for the I-knew-it smile to spread across their face. Then, she would add, *Three years apart* and watch smugness fade away.

*

In Wrightsville, it is easy to tell us apart. I am the inept one. It's not that I can't hold my own in the kitchen. I'm a decent cook, but compared to my siblings, my culinary skills and knowledge are negligible.

*

I've been on a dessert kick, having recently made a chocolate flourless torte, mocha cheesecake, dark chocolate and raspberry cheesecake, and peanut butter mousse. Cheesecake, I've decided, suits me perfectly. It can't be rushed. Even when cheesecake is done, it isn't really done. It's important to resist the temptation to pull it out and admire your efforts. Instead, wedge a wooden spoon in the oven door to prop it open for the heat to leak out slowly. Less chance of cracking. Holly taught me that.

*

I prefer to cook alone and uninterrupted, whereas my siblings thrive on the energy of others. I admire their ability to create in the midst of chaos. It seems to sharpen their senses and tighten their focus, whereas I unravel and lose my way. I am not well adapted to the frenetic pace but allow myself to be pulled along in this messy current of siblionic love.

39

*

Our spouses rarely intrude into these choppy waters. They'll venture forth only to pull out a child who has drifted too far into the deep.

*

Once more, dangerously high piles of bowls and utensils have washed up on the countertop. Warily, I extract a zester. Metal teeth laced with lemon grin up at me. I toss it into the sink and watch its flashy smile disappear.

*

Beef fajitas. Crème brûlée.

*

As John charges between the chicken in the kitchen and the grill on the back deck, sleepy limes awaken. They bob along, surfing the laminate lake. Wide-mouthed glasses, rimmed with chunky flakes of salt, grumble to be filled.

*

My brother allows me to prepare the peppers for the fajitas, showing me how to slice them with his knife. In this order: bottoms first, tops cut off, and then quartered. His knife slips through the skin like butter. I make a note to sharpen my knives, which cut like spoons, when I return home.

Later, my brother will swish around the back porch like a flamenco dancer. He'll celebrate lovely charred skins, snapping tongs in the air like castanets. He'll carefully remove the peppers at just the right moment, red and green coats glistening.

*

I need to perform an intervention, John proclaims five times during our dinner preparations. The first and second time, my sister follows him out to the back deck. They return, speaking in excited tones.

Don't do it, Holly warns.

But I want to help the guy! he retorts. *Come on!* He heads back outside, and my sister follows. I stay behind to keep an eye on the boiling pasta.

The third time he rumbles, *I need to perform an intervention. Stop me!* I leave the pasta draining in the colander to see what all the fuss is about.

My siblings are unabashedly spying on some hapless guy who is grilling shrimp two porches over, one story down. Deep concern lines their faces.

Such a shame, my sister clucks, craning her neck over the wooden railing.

My Lord! exclaims my brother. *Would you look at how he's overcooked them!*

Shhh! I say, worried Shrimp Guy might hear us. But he is oblivious to our presence, completely focused on the tiny bodies of shrimp littering his grill.

Whispering loudly, my sister says, *Look at him ruining perfectly good shrimp!*

I don't get it, I say, leaving them to peer over the railing. I return to the kitchen, thinking how shrimp is one of those rare words—like sheep and deer—that retains its form whether it's singular or plural. Shrimp and sheep dance with deer in my head until my brother waltzes over and taps me on the shoulder. *He should have skewered them instead of turning them over one by one like he is doing,* he explains. *That's just ridiculous.*

*

I look down at the colander. Renegade strands of pasta have curled themselves into a golden nugget. I scoop out the slimy clump with my fingers. My sister stares at her phone. My brother, pounding thickness out of a chicken breast, mutters, *I don't know where his head is at.*

His head is right here, my sister laughs and thrusts the phone under my brother's nose and then mine. I squint at a grainy picture. Shrimp Guy and his allegedly ruined shrimp hover over sudsy water. *See?* she says tapping a disapproving finger at her phone screen. *This guy has kept his shrimp on the grill for far too long.*

I don't see how you can tell that, I say, squinting harder at little white dashes I assume are the skewerless shrimp.

See how they are curled beyond the horseshoe shape? she says. *He should have taken them off the grill when they reached the* u *state. Now they are almost complete* o*'s. It's a sin what he's doing to that shrimp.* My sister seems to be speaking a foreign language.

I say, *Did you ever think maybe it's wrong to take pictures of people without their consent?*

What that guy is doing to the shrimp is far worse, retorts my sister.

Agreed, says my brother.

All this talk of shrimp and vowels is making my head swirl. How come I never knew about this shrimp and vowels thing? I sympathize with Shrimp Guy. I bet he's never thought of shrimp in terms of vowels either.

*

If pressed, I'd lean more on the side of shrimp being more consonant than vowellike. A *j* is more fitting of shrimp than a *u* or an *o*. Maybe I'm just taking this stance because I'm irked about not being in the know about shrimp and vowels. Am I bitter? These musings are drowned out by my brother's voice.

Come on! Let's see if he's removed the shrimp yet. A furtive glance passes between my siblings, and once more, they traipse outside.

I wonder if Shrimp Guy senses a piece of himself missing, that he has become an unknowing victim of my sister's habit of snapping up the world. Laughter drifts into the kitchen. Feeling like an accomplice in an unnamed crime, I wash a spoon, attempting to rinse Shrimp Guy from my mind.

*

While we were sleeping, the ocean fashioned a long ledge that stretches along the coastline. A mini cliff of sorts. My brother is already here, has carved out a spot for us, having set up beach chairs in a pleasing u-shaped manner that opens to the sea. Shaded by two umbrellas, the low-slung chairs ripple as one striped vowel.

*

My brother bakes in the sun. Hunched over a section of the ledge with a child's shovel, he notches out stairs of sand. He removes the soft and sandy crown, exposing a damp mix below. He levels off three tiers, dusting each to perfection. The finish is flawless, as if he had rolled out fondant and draped it artfully over the stairs.

*

Older beach patrons, who find the ocean's ledge too precarious of a drop, frequent his steps. His best customer is a woman who wears a flowered swim cap. Skin dangles from her legs, which poke out like fishing poles beneath her latex-sheathed hull. From her suit and fingers, she drips water upon his masterpiece.

She compliments my brother on his work, and he bows deeply with one arm tucked beneath his belly. The woman smiles, leaving a piping of watery pearls in her wake. My brother drops to one knee and repairs the edge of stairs that have crumbled.

*

To my son, he says, *You should bring your grandchild here someday. Show them these steps.* He waves an arm magnanimously over his work. *You tell them, 'My Uncle John built these stairs!'*

My son eyes his uncle suspiciously and then runs over to the tide pool that will soon disappear.

*

It won't be long before the tide comes in to claim his work.

*

Come on! John's fond of saying. He says this while he bastes a chicken or seasons a steak with one hand, the other arm outstretched, waiting for Holly or me to place the correct utensil, pan, or ingredient into his waiting hand.

Come on, kids! he says, rounding our children up on the last day of vacation and leading them toward the beach. *We need to see the sunrise and take pictures for Nan and Papa Joe.*

The children march obediently behind him. This is the best they have behaved all week. He has promised them each a dollar if they sit still for his camera. *It is,* he will later say, *the best investment he has ever made.*

*

Come and get your dolla! John shouts, tossing the *r* and five one dollar bills up into the sky. The children dash toward the flurry of flat inky bellies scuttling through the air. The day erupts with jubilant shouts as the children seize the green bodies, crumpling them in their sandy fists. When they also scatter, my brother stands alone under the cerulean sky.

*

John settles down into a beach chair. He wipes the sweat from his brow and begins to read. A few minutes later, he looks up and taps the cover of his book, *Patience: The Art of Peaceful Living. I need to work on this,* he says. His furrowed brow, and

45

the intensity in which he turns the pages, keeps me from laughing.

After ten minutes, my brother can hold back no longer. He rises from the chair, remembering he has one more thing to do. The ocean, too, begins to rise.

Beachy Cilantro Salsa

Yields about 1 ½ cups

Next time we go to the beach house, I'm making this dip for everyone. It is inspired by a recipe published decades ago in *Good Housekeeping*. It was (and still may be) served by a restaurant in New Jersey called East Bay Crab and Grille. The original didn't call for harissa paste. I also think it called for malt vinegar and some salt, but it's salty enough for my taste with using either hot sauce or harissa.

— *2 bunches of cilantro, rinsed and drained*
— *4 scallions, cut into several pieces*
— *3 teaspoons harissa paste*
— *3 tablespoons olive oil*
— *2 splashes (about 2 ½ tablespoons) red wine vinegar*
— *2 tablespoons lemon juice*
— *4 tablespoons water*

1. Put the cilantro and scallions in the food processor and pulse to chop roughly. If you don't have a food processor, use a knife to coarsely chop these ingredients.
2. In a bowl, stir all the other ingredients together. Add the cilantro mix and stir to combine.
3. Serve with pita chips or crostini.

Shark

I START THINKING about the game my brother, sister, and I played as children, where one of us is the shark and the other two run up the two steps of the wooden slide.

The slide, our ship, has deadly-spaced steps, not yet recalled as a strangulation hazard. Right now, it's the safest boat we know, anchored under the arch between the dining room and family room.

We stand on deck and then glide down the plank into the orange shag sea that is infested with a shark and wing-tipped piranha, the size of our father's shoes.

Three white cushions, vinyl islands of refuge, wander the waves. We must swim or jump to safety. If we get caught by the shark, we become the shark.

Game over, we put the islands away. Each clutching a cushion's handle, we stride through the airport as an announcement booms for everyone to wash their hands.

On our way to Timbuktu, we wave to our mother, who is dishing up Hamburger Helper, briefcases of secret files swinging at our sides.

Zucchini Helper Pie

Serves 4

This pretty dish works well for both breakfast and dinner.

— *3 cups zucchini, shredded*
— *1 cup parmesan, shredded or grated*
— *1 red onion, diced*
— *2 garlic cloves, minced*
— *1 large egg*
— *½ cup canola oil*
— *1 cup Bisquick biscuit mix*
— *2 teaspoons pepper*
— *1 teaspoon red pepper flakes*

1. Preheat the oven to 350 degrees.
2. Combine all the ingredients except for the biscuit mix. Then mix in the Bisquick.
3. Pour into a pie pan.
4. Bake for 45 minutes or until golden brown.

We Name Things

One: Moose

WHEN I AM seven, I rename us. My sister hates her name. *Why do you get to name us?* she wants to know. So, I make up my own saying: *I'm the oldest, so I make the rules.* This keeps her quiet for a while.

Moose are solitary creatures, unlike my sister, who is really more deer than moose. When we grow up, even though we share the same forest, we'll see only flashes of her. My sister and her buck will build a stunning house in the woods, surrounded by a canopy of oaks and hickories. She'll have herds of friends When her fawn bleats, she'll feed him cotton candy.

In Algonquin, moose means eater of twigs. Once plentiful, moose moved through Michigan and Massachusetts woods, munching willow, aspen, and oak. As forests were cleared for farming and logging, the moose left us. They have been making their way back home ever since.

Two: Posh Puffs

MY BROTHER IS Posh Puffs. Two years old, he doesn't care that he's named after a cubed box of tissues. It is, after all, *the softest way to treat a sore nose.*

It is the 1970s, and Posh Puffs come in four colors: strawberry, lemon, lime, and my favorite, blueberry. I love looking at the lady on the box with her blue profile and a cascade of berried hair tumbling down her neck. A small thrill escapes me each time I pull a blue puff from the top. Sometimes I blow my nose, and other times, I press the blue to my cheek. I make sure to keep the box beautiful, my fingers fanning the spray of tissue just so, as if I had never touched it.

Over dinner, my mother tells us how, shortly after our brother was born, he turned blue. *Diagnosed with hyaline membrane*, she says.

Hyaline comes from the Greek word *hyalos,* meaning glass. Each time my mother tells the story, I see her blue boy, his body shuddering as air drags like stone, threatening to skip across the pond of his heart and shatter glass lungs.

My brother is his own color now. He flies into town this week with his wife and three children. His skin is tanned from skiing. For the first time, I notice his brown hair is marbled with gray. Posh Puffs falls asleep on the couch; his breath rumbles the house. As his wife flips through *Martha Stewart Living*, the children eat blueberries and strawberries draining in a white colander.

Watching them, I wonder what our greats used to mop their noses. My grandfather used man-sized Kleenex. He always kept an extra box in the back of his Buick, just in case. Each time he turned a corner, the long box slid along the shelf under the rear window.

Three: Barbed Wire and Electricity

CHASED BY MOOSE, I sprint up the stairs and down the narrow hallway. Crossing the threshold to my bedroom, I whiz around, press the strike plate attached to the doorjamb, and shout, *Barbed wire and electricity!*

Moose halts, looking me in the eye. Pacing back and forth, she snorts and then gallops away.

I throw myself on the bed and read *The Sign of the Twisted Candles* or maybe *The Mystery at Lilac Inn*. After a while, I play a record. Sitting crisscross applesauce with *You Light Up My Life* on winged knees, I study the profile of Debby Boone singing into the microphone, dusting the cover with her powder-blue blazer and feathered bangs. I sing along. *So many nights, I'd sit by my window ...*

Then I sing "Da Doo Ron Ron" while running my finger over the magnetic force of Shaun Cassidy's impenetrable, cardboard smile. One day, we'll meet. I'll light up his life, and we'll marry.

After a while, bored, I drag Tickle deodorant with its big, wide ball under my pits, hairless except for a few wispy strands. I look in the mirror, pop a pimple on my nose, and brush my eyebrows with a tiny comb to get the Brooke Shields look.

I deactivate the force field and reenter the world.

Part Four: Wild Pig

MY SISTER COMPLAINS that I don't have a nickname too. *Don't worry*, I tell her. *I'm Wild Pig.*

Thinking back on this moment, I can't imagine why, of any name I could choose, I pronounced myself Wild Pig. As the oldest child, I'm reliably un-wild and not much for huddling. With more than two million sweat glands, I sweat way more than any pig. I hadn't yet stumbled across June Carter crooning, *When we was a courting / He called me sugar pie / Now he calls me other names / It's root, hog, or die ...*

*

The red carpet in the corner of the fourth-grade classroom has not been rolled out for my classmates and me, so we are not yet sitting on this swatch of a small, welcoming country, Yadi Wang and Louie Dreon pressing in on both sides of me as Ms. Boline reads us *Charlotte's Web*. When she gets to the chapter where Charlotte whispers *goodbye* to Wilbur, the pig, she will rise from her chair and say in a quivery voice, *Excuse me, children.* But she has not yet risen, nor parted the red sea to reach the Kleenex box at the far island of her desk. We have yet to learn that day's lesson: that it's okay for great leaders to cry over spiders.

*

At age seven, I have already written my first poem. It's a terrible poem about a flower and how it grows like the love I have for my mother. My mother loves the poem, or at least pretends to, and displays it on a shelf. So, I continue to write. Pigs, like poets, are inquisitive. They like to get at what is underneath the surface, break up and loosen crusted facts. I write a series of turtle poems, trying to know what is hidden under the shell.

*

Decades later, I root out this fact: On March 3, 1788, my fifth great-grandfather, Abraham Tourtillott, was elected hog reeve of Sudbury (now Bangor), Massachusetts. Having no idea what a hog reeve does, I dig some more.

Given that the townsmen voted that *hogs shall run at large, being well yoked*, it makes sense that somebody should find the swine that stray and destroy gardens. As hog reeve, my great put rings in the noses of pigs whose owners had neglected this duty. For every hog the hog reeve reeved, he received four shillings.

I sniff and tug out the roots to the word reeve, its origins sunk in the *riff* of sheriff.

Maybe our cells house memories of our ancestors? Maybe I chose Wild Pig because on some cellular level I knew my fifth great-grandfather was once a policer of pigs. Abraham was also elected collector, surveyor of roads, and church warden. He was not selected for the fish committee or culler of staves. One person can only do so much. If he had been, I would have proclaimed myself Fish, and Wild Pig would never have existed. Or perhaps, Culler of Lumber might have romped around with Moose and Posh Puffs.

Wild Piggies

Serves 8

My husband does most of the grocery shopping, and the three ingredients for this recipe often make their way into his cart. This bite-size appetizer is perfect for parties, Super Bowl, March Madness, and binge-watching *Murdoch Mysteries*. If you don't like the wild look, use a pizza cutter to slice the dough and cheese.

— *1 tube crescent rolls (8 ounces)*
— *1 package of miniature smoked sausage links (14 ounces)*
— *4 slices cheese (American or cheddar)*

1. Preheat oven to 375 degrees. Line a baking sheet with parchment.
2. Unroll the crescent rolls. Tear each perforated triangle into 4 or 5 pieces. Tear off small pieces of cheese and place on top of each tattered blanket.
3. Place a sausage on one end of a cheese-sheeted blanket, roll it up, and place it on baking sheet. Repeat with the remaining sausages. (You will probably have some leftover.)
4. Bake until the blankets are golden, which is about 10 minutes.

My mother always had something up her sleeve

IN THE 1970S, when I am ten, my magician mother pulls a baking sheet out of a canary yellow cabinet. My brother, sister, and I, her eager assistants, lean into the Formica countertop, watching as she *thunks* down raw meat and molds it into a teardrop. Because I am the oldest, I get to push eyes of black olives into its cold skin. My sister names this hedgehog Fred. We pierce his body with slivered almonds. We are amateurs—the coverage spotty, the crunchy quills askew.

Hedgehogs are lactose intolerant. A group of hedgehogs is not considered a herd, but an array or prickle. When Saint Sebastian was tied to a tree and showered with arrows for being a Christian, it's written that his body was *full of arrows as an urchin*. Back then, urchin meant hedgehog. Unlike the hedgehog, when scared, Sebastian did not roll into a ball and tuck himself away.

As my mother carries Fred to the oven, we palm our misgivings. My mother opens the oven door and bows. That is our cue to run outside. For forty-five minutes at 350, we fly around like birds until my mother calls us to the table. With sleight of hand, she set a golden, spiny-coated Fred before us. My father appears, and we all change into carnivores.

Hedgy Meatloaf

Serves 3 to 4

My husband says his mom makes the best meatloaf. She puts milk in hers. So, to make him happy, I splash in a bit of milk.

— *1 ½ pounds ground beef*
— *1 onion, finely chopped*
— *2 garlic cloves, minced*
— *1 egg, beaten*
— *¼ cup Italian breadcrumbs*
— *½ cup barbecue sauce (I use Sweet Baby Ray's Honey Chipotle)*
— *¼ cup milk*
— *Slivered or sliced almonds and 3 black olives (optional)*

1. Preheat oven to 375 degrees.
2. Mix all the ingredients together. Put them into a greased meatloaf pan. Drizzle some additional barbecue sauce over the top. Spread the sauce with the back of a spoon.

    Note: If you prefer a hedgier look to your loaf, place the mixture on a broiler rack and mold into a hedgehog shape instead of using a loaf pan. To create a prickly coat, press some almonds into the meat. Insert 2 olives for eyes and 1 for the nose.

3. While the meatloaf bakes, go outside and play. Take it out when the meat is done after 50 to 60 minutes.

4. Drain the grease and serve.

Mango Jesus

EVER SINCE MY sister bought her iPhone, I've been bombarded with irrelevant, obtuse references to nothing in particular.

Almost daily, she sends pictures of her two-year-old son, King. She occasionally intersperses cryptic messages and photos of something else. Lately, I've received a rash of myself or, more accurately, parts of myself—my bare foot, my yawning mouth, and part of my ear. Pieces of myself I do not recall giving away.

One time, I caught her in the act. We were eating bagels or rolls—I don't recall exactly what—and it had poppy seeds, one of which lodged between my teeth. As I slipped my pinky into my mouth, attempting to rake out the annoying seed, my sister snapped a picture. With my fingernail still wedged between teeth, my words came out muddy. *Wha' did you jus' do?*

Nnn-noo-thing, Holly stuttered through spurts of laughter.

Let me see that, I said and reached for her phone. She jerked it away but was thoughtful enough to turn it around so I could view the screen.

Before I had my bearings, I briefly thought that instead of looking at a close-up of my teeth, complete with poppy poop, I was looking at a bowling ball lodged between spare pins. Holly hugged the phone to her chest and then snuck a peek of my teeth displayed on her screen, causing her to chortle like a rabid chicken.

Delete it, I demanded. *I don't want my miniature teeth, with or without poppy seeds, to be out there.*

I just did, she snorted.

You deleted it?

Yes.

Though she was still cackling when I left, I chose to believe her.

*

She has titled today's email "Self."

Before I open this, or any of her emails, I amuse myself by playing a little game. I read Holly's subject line and begin guessing what the subject matter is *really* about. This isn't as easy as it sounds. I say the word aloud. *Self. Self. Self,* hoping to stumble into the correct answer. Hmm. Holly's entering day two of being sick and holed up with an ear infection. *Self.* I've got it. She's snapped a picture of her sick self. I imagine her splayed upon the couch, a blanket pulled up around her shoulders. I'm going to win this one.

But I am wrong. "Self" is her son, King, in a highchair, inspecting a half-naked orange that he must have peeled him*self.* Self is not her. It's him. My sister may not be logical, but she is selfless. Self, in her world, is not her. It never is.

*

She's into peeling lately. She sent a link to "How Jesus Would Peel a Mango." The subject heading was "LOL." I guessed correctly that she thought something was laughing out loud funny. I watched the clip on YouTube. It's just some guy—his hands, actually—cutting into a mango. That's about it. While it's not offensive, neither is it funny. It's just boring, but apparently, Holly found it so hysterical she posted a link to it on her blog—a blog, by the way, which I am not permitted to read. *I need to feel free to write whatever I want,* she has told me whenever I have asked for the link. I've stopped asking.

*

We met up for happy hour at our parents' home a few days later.

Did you watch the clip? she inquired.

Yes.

And? I could tell from the way her eyebrows twitch that she was holding back a laugh so we could laugh together.

And it isn't funny.

Yes, it is.

No. It's really not.

Okay, my sister said. I thought she was about to reconsider. Instead, she pulled out her phone and made me watch it all over again. This time, she narrated the whole thing.

Notice how he is in a garage, she said, pointing her finger and blotting out the Jesus man who is cutting the mango. *Jesus,* she explained, *was a carpenter, and this guy*—she giggled—*This guy is in a garage. It's perfect.*

Call me a dullard, but I didn't see the connection between Jesus and garages.

I pulled out my reading glasses to magnify this diminutive mango world. Perhaps I was missing something.

See? See right there? He's slicing the mango into the shape of a cross. She grabbed her belly and tried not to laugh. *See, he's doing it again! He's holding it out now, offering it to you.* She cast me a sideways, expectant look. Her body started to twitch.

It's not funny, I said.

You just don't understand subtle humor.

Subtle? It's so subtle that it's not even there. It is not funny.

With shoulders trembling, Holly emitted a series of staccato squeals. King toddled up to her and furrowed his face. He looked alarmed. Who could blame him? His mother's face had turned magenta, and she doubled over like she was passing a kidney stone. When she finally rose, tears were dancing down her face. She exploded with laughter.

I can't even describe her laugh. It is terribly infectious. King looked noticeably relieved. His brow smoothed; he thrust his head back and hooted loudly, attempting to mimic his mother. Holly only laughed harder. I started to laugh, and before long, we were all laughing so hard that I had to run to the bathroom before I peed my pants.

Just thinking about Holly laughing out loud, especially about something as unfunny as the Jesus clip, has me laughing again. It's not funny. At all. She just has that effect on people.

*

Unlike my sister, I attach subject titles that are germane to the content of my communications. Take this one for example.

My subject heading is "Sweet Conversation Overheard." The content was as follows:

Hi, Holly. Tom and his friend, Brady, are playing in the living room. I'm in the dining room. This is what I overhear:

"Hey, Brady. You want to see some new ministers?" (I assume, though can't see, that Tom is rummaging through his dad's mail for a church bulletin.)

"What's a minister?"

"A minister is someone who preaches."

"Preaches?"

"Teaches you about Jesus."

Silence. Then, "Tom, do you think Jesus is really real?"

"Yes."

"He's probably not living right now, right?"

"Jesus is. He's probably living in Heaven."

"Yeah."

In my sister's world, Jesus is lurking in someone's garage.

*

My brother—who lives in North Carolina and didn't find Jesus peeling a mango funny either—sent out an email yesterday with the subject line, "Guess who gotta hair cut while mamma is gone?" I click on the photo and erupt into laughter. On a white bathroom countertop, scrawled out in hairy brown letters, is *W i L L*. I'm laughing because this is funny. I envision my brother, slouched over the bathroom countertop, his long fingers neatly arranging his son's freshly clipped hair into a demented, hairy looking version of his name. He is too absorbed in the creation of his furry sculpture to respond to his son's repeated inquiry into what he is doing. Eventually, my brother thrusts his hand out and says, *Will, grab my camera, please.*

I feel a bit bad for my sister-in-law. She's in some hotel in Idaho, and this is the scene that greets her when she opens her email. Her son's name spelled out in his own locks. No picture is attached of what he looks like now after daddy cut his hair. I feel guilty that I can't stop laughing.

The shaggy *i* in *W i L L* reminds me of the steamy hairball I accidentally stepped on yesterday morning. If I were my sister, I would have taken a picture of the bottom of my foot streaked with cat yak and emailed it to three hundred of my closest friends. Maybe even posted it on my blog, if I had a blog.

*

I shouldn't be so hard on my sister. There was that time she picked my son up from school when he had a half day and fired off a series of emails with attached photos that matched their subject title. First was "Got him" with a corresponding photo of Tom in the backseat of her car with King. An hour later came "Cheese," and it was a picture of Tom eating grilled cheese. Fifteen minutes after that came "What's left?" It was a still life of a splotch of hardened cheese and a nibbled rind of bread crust on a green plate. I braced myself for the next subject. "Look what I did!" I decided she had sent me a photo of a bird's-eye view of a toilet bowl that contained my son's droppings. It turned out to be Tom and King, arm in arm, standing proudly before a tower of blocks.

She broke her sense-making streak by hurling an enigmatic email titled "Or."

I lost that game too. "Or" in my sister's world turned out to be a snapshot of trees. In the foreground is dappled grass. *Or?* I wondered. *Or what?* Above the picture, she had typed to apparently clarify the *or. Turn around and see this … cabin left at ten o'clock.*

Turn around where? What cabin? Left from whose point of view? Maybe she was referencing the cabin in her husband's family that I was not supposed to know about. The one in the northern Leelanau Peninsula that she and her family occasionally slipped away to for weekend getaways.

How long have you had this cabin? I asked when my mother alluded to it.

None of your business, my sister said as she threw my mother a glare.

My mother mouthed back, *Sorry.*

Why? I asked Holly. *Are you running some secret operation out of it?*

No.

Why not tell me then?

Because you would show up.

To your secret cabin?

Yes, and you'd drag your whole family with you.

I've never shown up somewhere I wasn't invited to.

Oh, but you would if you could.

No, I wouldn't.

Yes, you would.

We live only three miles from each other, I reminded her. *Never once have I shown up on your doorstep uninvited.*

But you could.

But I don't.

You can stop by, she said. *Whenever. I'd love that.*

Well, I won't. Just like I won't drive five hours to your cabin unannounced.

Six.

What?

It's six hours to get there. But I'm not telling you how to get there. I don't want you just showing up.

She will never tell me where this cabin is, just like she won't tell where her blog exists.

I think about how funny it would be to uncover the location of her secret cabin. Just to rile her, I might drive six hours and show up unannounced, family in tow. I'm grinning so hard my face hurts.

*

Freshman year of college, I signed up for a Logic & Reasoning class and quickly felt like a victim of a bait-and-switch scheme. Week after week, I entered a foreign land where the professor spoke complete gibberish. I barely passed the class and blamed my grade on poor teaching, but now, over twenty years later, it occurs to me that maybe it was me. While I consider myself to be more logical than my sister, this is like saying the Brachiosaurus was bigger than the seventy-five-foot

Apatosaurus. If it took me decades to arrive at this insight into me, my Self with a capital S, what else am I missing? I worry what it is that I do that could be considered odd.

My husband would know. During dinner, I feel him out about it. *Honey?*

Mm, hmm, he replies, chewing his steak.

I've been thinking about, well, you know how my sister is a prolific sender of cryptic emails, and we now learn that my brother has a penchant for scrawling words out with hair. So, I'm wondering, what odd thing do I do. Or, I hear a hopeful note creep into my voice, *maybe I don't do anything strange?*

You have to admit, your brother is pretty damn funny. This is all he says. We both start laughing.

I married a man who is quite logical. And direct. After watching some guy in a garage slice a mango, my husband, without laughing, emailed Holly. *You need to get a hobby,* he wrote.

My sister and I both thought that was funny.

WWJD Mango Smoothie

Serves 3 to 4

WWJD Mango Smoothies are the mainstay of our house.
WWJD stands for What Would Jesus Drink? Here's a helpful
hint. When bananas on your counter turn brown, make a habit
of peeling them, breaking them into several pieces, and tossing
them into a freezer bag. That way, you'll always have this
ingredient handy.

— *1 ¾ cup (about 16 ounces) low-fat vanilla yogurt*
— *1 cup frozen mango chunks*
— *½ cup frozen fruit (blueberries, pineapple, raspberries, or blackberries work well)*
— *½ frozen banana*
— *A splash of orange juice*

1. Put all ingredients into a food processor or blender.
2. Blend until smooth.

A Nod to Ernest Borgnine

WE WERE IN the car headed to breakfast when a piece aired on NPR about Ernest Borgnine.

I thought Borgnine was dead, said my husband. *Ninety-four years old. Imagine that.*

Mermaid Man! shouted our five year old, thoroughly impressed with this credential of being the voice behind the over-the-hill superhero in the SpongeBob SquarePants cartoon.

Puss, I was thinking. *That is it. Puss.*

In the interview, he referred to his face as a *puss. Ugly puss,* I think he said. Or something to the effect of not liking to see his puss on screen. Even though it was the radio, I could see Ernest Borgnine's round, craggy face, proclaiming the old-fashioned word in that unmistakable, gravelly voice of his. I could see it slipping out between the gap in his top front teeth. *P-U-S-S.* I wanted to hail him for hauling out this outdated slang to reference his face.

I didn't know *puss* was the word I was searching for to finish my latest poem until Borgnine tossed it like a life buoy over the airwaves to me. *Puss.* So perfect. My entire body was humming to finish the poem. As we pulled into the restaurant parking lot, I considered asking my husband to turn around and go home. But he and my son were already scrambling out of the car in anticipation of feeding their hungry bellies. Declaring my desire to return home to finish a poem wouldn't go over well.

What are you thinking about? my husband asks, biting into his bagel.

Puss, I say.

Puss? he replies.

Yes, puss. A severe-looking woman at the next table shoots me a disapproving glance. I ignore her. *Hello?! Ernest Borgnine?* I remind him of the segment we heard in the car. *I tell you, the minute he said* puss *it struck me that that was the word I needed to finish my poem.*

I wouldn't use puss, he says, lowering his voice.

No?

No. Puss? Come on … It conjures up … Well, you know …

I realize what he is getting at. I look over at our son, quite absorbed in his blueberry bagel. I lean into my husband and softly whisper, *I thought you liked puss.*

I do, but not in a poem.

From the way the woman in the next booth over shifts uncomfortably, I don't think she likes puss under any condition.

I am not swayed. I am committed to puss.

For the rest of breakfast, all things Ernest Borgnine run through my head. I think of his puss first. For a man I hadn't seen for years—mistakenly thought, as had my husband, that he was dead—it is surprisingly easy to conjure up his face.

Two things immediately come to mind. Bushy eyebrows that could easily be mistaken for two caterpillars curled comfortably above smiling eyes. What actor today has such bushy eyebrows? None offhand that I can think of. And even if there are, how many feel that free to let them grow wild like that? The other feature is the gap in the middle of his top front teeth. It is rather sweet and gives off the impression that he is approachable and friendly.

I had a gap between my top two front teeth. Bigger than Borgnine's, a small car could have passed through and still had room to spare. At least it felt that way. Fortunately for me and my self-esteem, I got braces in fifth grade, and the gap eventually disappeared.

It was in my early teens that I saw *Marty* on television. What I remember about the movie is that my tongue hurt from flicking it ragged between metal braces to inspect any gap closing progress while I watched Borgnine play some guy with a gap between his teeth. My mother said that *Marty* was originally shown in movie theaters sometime in the 1950s and that he had won some award for his performance. An Academy Award, I think. I should see if I can get my hands on a DVD of *Marty* at the library.

Growing up, I caught a few reruns of Borgnine playing McHale in *McHale's Navy*. The television show always started with a ship sweeping across the ocean and Ernest Borgnine on deck, smiling. He always seemed to be smiling out from under those shaggy caterpillars.

Breakfast is over, and we get back in the car and head home. I start thinking about that time in college when I discovered I had a knack for impersonating Ethel Merman.

Mom's thinking about her poem, my husband says to the rearview mirror image of our son, allowing his eyes to briefly tear away from traffic and take in his silent wife. I must admit, usually he is spot on with identifying my thinking-about-a-poem look. This look must come off the same as my thinking-about-Ethel-Merman look. *I am going to finish that poem when I get home,* I announce. My husband grins, thinking he's pegged me once again.

Back to Ethel. I was in my dorm room, trying to stay awake while studying for next day's midterms. In danger of falling asleep, I belted out the Ethel Merman song, "There's No Business Like Show Business" and was roused to my toes. It's a nifty trick. You should try it sometime. Just remember to drink in generous amounts of air, add a healthy dose of vibrato, and clip the ends of each word crisply as you boom it out. So, it sounds like: *there's nooo buuusiness like shooooow buuusiness like nooo buuusiness I knooow* ... If you're trying to stay awake, "Everything's Coming Up Roses" works too, but, for whatever reason, not quite as well. Thanks to Ethel, I aced all my exams.

Thus ensued my brief infatuation with Ethel Merman. It didn't last long. I was home on break and performed my newly discovered talent for imitating Ethel Merman. That's when my mother told me that Ethel had recently died. She remarked that Ethel had once been married to Borgnine, her fourth and final husband. For reasons she couldn't recall, the marriage didn't last long.

We return home, and I promptly get to work on my poem that I've titled "The Winter of 2011." The poem is about getting satisfaction from kicking off dirty snow chunks that grow at shockingly rapid rates underneath motor vehicles in wintertime. These self-breeding ice chunks are the kudzu of the North. At some point, they crack off here and there, in parking lots and driveways. When you have an armful of groceries, you stumble over one of these unsightly turds and drop your keys in a pile of snow.

I change *face* to *puss* and realize I must also replace *ugly* with *lowdown*. The sixth stanza now reads:

How is it—
after kicking your
lowdown puss—

My God. I *love* it. Puss is perfect. It rescues the stanza from mediocrity, elevating the entire poem to another level. I am ecstatic. If I had Ernest Borgnine's phone number, I'd call and thank him for helping me finish this poem. A phone call would be a bit presumptuous. A letter might be better.

Dear Mr. Borgnine,

I apologize on behalf of my husband and myself for thinking you were dead. For selfish reasons, I am so glad you are not. Were it not for you, I would not have completed my poem. (See enclosed.) How generously, and without fanfare, you sent me puss. Thank you for resurrecting such a quaint, old-fashioned word.

Your newest fan,
Jennifer Clark
P.S. I'm sorry about your marriage to Ethel not working out.

I envision him opening the letter, and the gap in his teeth is evident as he smiles. But it wanes when he gets to the part about his ex-wife. I delete that line and wonder what other actor goes around with gaps in their teeth these days? Lauren Hutton.

But she was born in 1943 and has, in my estimation, a more modest space between her teeth compared to Borgnine.

I am shocked to find how easy it is to obtain Borgnine's address. In one click, I am on a site that not only announces his Beverly Hills address but promises to reveal secrets that will get Ernest Borgnine to respond to my letter if I go to this other link. I don't. I'm becoming a bit suspicious of the site since it has posted an outdated photo—maybe taken twenty years ago—of the actor. It is the same Borgnine I invoked from my childhood. He comes across as a dapper bulldog, smiling and wearing a dark suit with a red hanky peeking out of the pocket. His tie boasts a spray of flowers, which picks up the same shade of red. His hair, with touches of gray, is still dark. If the picture is outdated, maybe the address is too.

I find things about him I didn't know, not that I'm the expert on Ernest Borgnine. Far from it. But I'm beginning to feel guilty for barely thinking about this guy since *McHale's Navy*, while he ends up single-handedly saving my poem.

Ernie is also a navy man in real life, a veteran of World War II. (I'm calling him Ernie now because in one of the stories I just read, it quotes him as saying he prefers Ernie over Ernest or Mr. Borgnine.)

I wonder what Ethel called him. She was number three of five wives. Really not much of a marriage since it lasted under two months. Makes you wonder what happened. In Ethel's memoir, she included a chapter titled "My Marriage to Ernest Borgnine" and offers up a blank page to the reader. Maybe Ernie's string of failed marriages had something to do with his parents separating when he was just the tender age of two. His mother whisked him off to Italy, but a few years later, his parents reunited and returned to Connecticut, his birthplace.

Upon reconciling, they decided to take the Italian out of their last name, changing it from *Borgino* to *Borgnine*. So, Ermes Effron Borgino became Ernest Borgnine, or Ernie for short.

This is interesting. Google Ernest Borgnine, and you come up with one hundred and sixteen thousand hits. Seems like a lot. However, google somebody famous who was born after 1970, and you'll discover that younger celebrities beat out the older ones. I base this statement on the one experiment I just did using Ashton Kutcher. Born in 1978, Kutcher has three million four hundred and seventy thousand hits. That's thirty times more than Ernie.

Is it just me or does it seem like a crime to have such a—I don't know what you'd call it—a cyber gap? At the very least it seems disrespectful that someone who has lived almost an entire century has their number of hits vastly exceeded by someone whose life has spanned three short decades and has starred in movies like, *Dude, Where's My Car?*

On the other hand, I think there is a larger, underlying truth in all this. A profusion of meaningless information is floating around out there. Take Kutcher, for example. I just got on his Twitter account—I've never been on anybody's Twitter account until this moment—and see that, as of today, he has made 6,472 tweets and over six million people are followers of comments like, *I FANCY the new UI on THE FANCY.* What the hell? I bet Ernie hasn't ever polluted cyberspace by tweeting.

How many cyber notations does one really need in this life? Even Ernie's one hundred and sixteen thousand is too much. Someone should set a limit. Say five, ten entries tops? Until then, I begrudgingly decide to partake in this gluttonous behavior.

Instead of mailing the letter to Ernie, I will figure out how to enhance his internet presence. Perhaps an addition to the Ernest Borgnine's entry in Wikipedia might do him justice. It's not much, but how I see it, it will help him get one step closer to Kutcher. I write the following email:

Dear Jimmy Wales,

If possible, could you please update Ernest Borgnine's current Wikipedia entry to include the following statement?

One of Borgnine's greatest accomplishments is something this actor didn't even realize he had accomplished! Unbeknownst to Ernie, by uttering the word puss *during a 2011 NPR interview, he inspired an obscure, relatively unknown poet to finish her poem, "Winter of 2011."*

Thanks to Ernie and this poem*, the term puss *quickly regained the relative popularity it once enjoyed. This resurgence in* puss *is evidenced by the fact that within months, Facebook officially changed its name to Pussbook.*

Thank you,
Jennifer Clark

P.S. **Please hyperlink the word* poem *to "The Winter of 2011." I have attached it for your convenience.*

Who am I kidding? I can't send this email. Even as I was writing it, I realized, except for the obscure poet reference, none of it is true. At least, not yet. Perhaps the best way I can pay homage to Ernie is to get my poem out. Start circulating it to a few select literary journals. But I don't.

Instead, I make a list of what Ernie and I have in common:

1. We both use the word puss.

2. I am now the age (minus five years) that Ernie was when I was born.

3. We both had a thing for Ethel Merman, but it didn't last long.

4. When Ernie and his caterpillar eyebrows were busy playing Stanislaus Katczinsky in the 1979 film *All Quiet on the Western Front*, I was busy using a tiny comb to shape my eyebrows into a Brooke Shields style that was all the rage that year.

After looking over the list, I realize it is a stretch. With the exception of the first entry, Ernie and I have nothing in common at all.

I should stop thinking about him. I pick up *Bon Appétit* and start browsing the recipes I am too intimidated to make. I wonder what magazines Ernie subscribes to. *Reader's Digest? Life Magazine?* Before his last wife died, I bet she had plenty of magazines like *Ladies' Home Journal* and *Redbook* scattered throughout the house. Now and then, he probably comes across one, thumbs through it and stops at the green bean casserole recipe that has been dog-eared. I can just see him pulling a man-size hanky out of his back pocket and mopping up tears that slip down his sweet, craggy puss.

I wonder how long he's been a widower. Whoops, my bad. Ernie's fifth wife—who he has been married to for over thirty-five years—is still alive and well. Tova Traesnaes was born in Norway in 1941. That's just two years shy of Lauren Hutton's 1943 birth. Turns out, Tova is quite the businesswoman. She's taken this face cream concocted with cactus that was made by a family in Mexico and sells it on QVC along with a host of other cosmetics. I hope the family gets a good cut out of the whole deal. I wonder if she sells those eyebrow combs that I used back in my teen years. Maybe I should start watching QVC and order some of her makeup. I can't remember the last time I bought makeup.

Get this. Lauren Hutton sells makeup too! Coincidence? I don't think so. And she has relatively plush eyebrows for a woman. Ethel Merman, on the other hand, had pencil thin eyebrows. One site described them as quizzical eyebrows. Maybe that outwardly thin-thick eyebrow difference was simply an outward manifestation of the differences between Ernie and Ethel. Maybe Ethel lifted her quizzical eyebrows one too many times, and Ernie said enough. A marriage ended over eyebrows. I'm sure it happens.

Okay, so I just got back from the library, and you know what? The Kalamazoo Public Library has two copies of *Marty*, and they are both checked out. The young man working the media area apologized and said I could place one on reserve. I was so relieved to know that Ernie was still vital and circulating that I almost forgot to thank the young man. I left, forgetting to place it on reserve.

So, I'm thinking about Ernie's eyebrows again. Seriously, who really wears eyebrows like that anymore? I don't know what it is about eyebrows, but they seem to have played an astonishingly large role in Ernie's life.

And it hits me. I've been thinking about Ernie's gap in terms of his teeth being disrupted by a *gap* rather than his gap being flanked by *teeth*. I wonder why.

Flank. Now that is one powerful word. Makes me want to write a poem right now, using the word flank in it. Or maybe a poem titled "Flank" or the bit more edgy "Flank You." I'll write it, send it off, and see what happens. And then I will give another nod to Ernie because I was led to write about flank from thinking about him. Who knew that an old man with caterpillar eyebrows could be such a source of inspiration?

I could easily become addicted to Ernie.

Breakfast Toast with Borgnine

Serves 8

Around the holidays, my son is always asking me to make this hearty French toast with its own built-in syrup.

— *1 loaf Texas toast, cut in half*
— *1 cup brown sugar*
— *½ cup butter*
— *1 teaspoon corn syrup*
— *6 eggs*
— *2 cups milk*
— *2 teaspoons vanilla*
— *3 teaspoons cinnamon*

1. Heat sugar, butter, and corn syrup in a saucepan. Stir often. When it's a syrup consistency, pour into a buttered 9 x 13 glass pan.
2. Arrange bread, crustless sides down, in two rows. Slices should overlap slightly, like fallen dominoes.
3. Whisk together the eggs, milk, vanilla, and cinnamon. Pour over the bread.
4. Cover in foil and refrigerate overnight.
5. In morning, preheat oven to 350 degrees. Bake until golden brown, about 40 minutes.

Open Letter to Milk Sitting Forlornly on Counter

Dear Milk,

 I'm sorry you sit all alone except for the crumbs left by toast taunting you, a reminder that you are not toast and that, despite your frothy promises, my son didn't even bring you to his lips. You probably feel bad, and I don't blame you. I know what you're thinking. My child's destiny for greatness lives and dies with you, and like all bad children who don't drink you, he will end up curling on couches like spineless isopods with spongy teeth. Then we, the bad, bad parents of this world will gnash our hard, hard teeth and weep.

 I've never admitted this before, but you have a kind of hold over me. I realize it every time I catch myself blathering on and bartering as if you were God calcified. *Finish your milk. Drink your milk. Have three more sips, and then you can have another cookie, a piece of cake, or do whatever you want. The world is your oyster.* Oyster shoyster. When will this madness stop, Milk? Since when did you become the litmus test for being a good parent? How long will I be consumed by belief that if my kid guzzles you, then he's practically a demigod, and I'm somehow made dazzling in the swilling?

 I don't like your attitude, Milk. You don't do my body any good. I can't tolerate you except for that brief stint when I was at the Women's Final Four and nine months pregnant with the very child who now refuses you. What a day that was! My mother's cousin's kid was on the Michigan State basketball team. Go Green! If someone on her team had gulped one more glass of milk, they might have won. At the after-party, they passed out ice cream, and I licked your relations like there was no lactose-free tomorrow. Behold my behind, Milk, not one teensy fart fluttered that day. It was divine.

But you don't care about any of that, do you? You skim the surface of life, sitting so low on the kitchen counter that you can't see what I see this morning. Know what that is? My boy is outside, dashing around the front yard and kicking a soccer ball instead of sitting on his butt and drinking you. I think he's doing his body good, don't you?

I want to smack your smug, congealing coat right off of you. Think this is the life, Milk? Has it even crossed that thin-membraned mind of yours of where you, oh Milk of Humble Beginnings, came from, slopping about the insides of a junkie mother cow whose one-day-old calf was probably ripped from her side, so she too could grow up to be shot up with who knows what? Only so parents like me can buy you, stuff you in a too-full refrigerator, lug you out, and pour you down the throats of our babes. Oh, don't give me that oh-look-at-me-I've-got-vitamin D! Your slick slogans won't work on me anymore.

What? Crying now? Waaa! Waaa! Is the truth a bit hard to digest? Why don't you go back to where you came from? Take your fortified, white ass and get the hell out of here. Got it, Milk? I got your number, and it is up. You and your milky mustache are going down. The drain, that is.

Happy trails,
Jennifer Clark

No Moo Gazpachoo

Serves 8

This cold soup is so pretty and refreshing to serve on a hot day.

— *6 large tomatoes, diced*
— *2 cucumbers, 1 peeled but both diced*
— *8 radishes*
— *3 red bell peppers, diced*
— *3 garlic cloves, minced*
— *4 carrots, chopped*
— *1 red onion, diced*
— *1 jalapeno, diced*
— *1 lemon, juiced*
— *2 tablespoons olive oil*
— *2 tablespoons red wine vinegar*
— *1 tablespoon red pepper flakes*
— *Salt for taste*
— *Cilantro for garnish*

1. In a blender or food processor, purée the first 8 ingredients until smooth. If you're feeling a bit daring,

pluck a few sprigs of cilantro and toss them in as well. You might need to purée in several batches.

2. Pour into a large container.

3. Mix in a pinch of salt, pepper flakes, lemon juice, olive oil, and red wine vinegar.

4. Cover and chill in refrigerator for at least 4 hours.

5. Serve cold, garnishing soup with cilantro.

Sample, anyone?

(Opening Day. November 12, 2014)

WITHIN MINUTES, MY sister has abandoned me, disappearing within the bowels of the one-hundred-and-forty-eight-thousand-square-foot Costco store that's just opened in Kalamazoo. The faithful have turned out in bulk to worship this new god in town. Giddy with delight, they roll their shopping carts up and down the aisles, past me, a non-believer who has not yet been anointed with the Costco spirit.

I make the best of it and stand in front of the Happy Light display, one of the estimated four thousand items the store carries. Savoring a free sample of Sanders Salted Caramel, I tilt my head back and absorb as much fake light as possible. The Gospel, according to Costco, notes happiness via this brilliantly lit display can be mine for one hundred dollars.

Before I can reach my happy place, my sister returns. *These lights*, Holly says, *are for people who suffer from seasonal affective disorder.*

I know what it's for, I snap. *These lights must be duds because their emissions aren't working at all.*

Obviously, Holly quips and flounces off in the direction of sacks of stacked dried rice, each the size of a small hippo.

I decide to give the Happy Lights a few more minutes to do their thing.

Even with my eyes closed, I feel overwhelmed, lost in a storm of metal shelving, a blizzard of cotton balls, and a gale of celestial globes not yet spinning beneath an artificial warehouse sky. Why did I let my sister talk me into shopping on opening day? Just being with Holly is an event; ladling on this visit overloads the senses.

Opening my eyes, I stare into the glow of promise. There isn't a light big enough to leach the growing storm of doubt forming in my bones. I allowed my sister to convince me to sign up not just for the fifty-five-dollar annual basic membership fee. *You've got to bump it up to the executive membership,* she said. *For a hundred and ten dollars, you'll get a two percent return on purchases you make throughout the year. You'll get your money back in no time. I did it, mom did it, and you should too.* How to reconcile that I belong to an elite club, part of the unhungry who crave all things in bulk while one in nine people are chronically hungry in this world?

I abandon the Happy Lights and go off in search of Holly.

Over time, I'll come to learn that Costco can be a fickle god, enticing with offerings that are there one day and gone the next and cultivating a buy-now-or-it-may-be-gone-tomorrow-and-you'll-be-sorry-for-life mentality. Costco also gets a kick out of putting disparate items together. One minute, you're looking at cauliflower crust frozen pizza and then, taking a couple of steps, you're confronted by a pair of jeans and fuzzy slippers. It's all a bit discombobulating, designed to force you to explore more of the store and snatch up things you don't really need.

But right now I am not that savvy as I forge through this forest of consumerism, a chorus of Roomba iRobots chanting in my ear.

Where is Holly? I start worrying that one of these shrink-wrapped pallets of gluten-free-you-name-it has toppled over and knocked her unconscious. Crap. That's probably why she hasn't returned. I have to find her.

The odds of getting hurt by falling organic quinoa on the left side and jars of Nutella on the right must be twice as great if you stroll down the middle of the aisle. To be safe, I walk along the edge of the aisle, hugging fat jars of olives that clamber up metal shelving like kalamata kudzu.

It might seem laughable, but later, I'll discover that these mega stores with their towering stacks of merchandise have spawned a new specialization: falling merchandise injury lawyers. In 2017, the Bureau of Labor Statistics reported 237 deaths as a result of being struck by falling objects or equipment while on the job in the United States. Who's keeping track of the shoppers' deaths?

I cautiously proceed further into the store. There she is. In the time we've been separated, she's become fast friends with a stranger who has her arm slung around the neck of a gigantic stuffed bear. Holly is taking the stranger's picture. Both the bear and the woman sport a thick, black mustache.

Holly says, *This is Kathleen Casey. As part of "Movember," she's bringing awareness to men's health. Isn't that wonderful?*

Unless she plans to buy the bear, I don't think it's wonderful. Who knows where that mustache has been? I attempt to be social, though, and join the conversation. *We grew up with a Kathleen Casey, but you're not Kathleen Casey,* I say.

I am Kathleen Casey.

Our Kathleen Casey was a girl scout, and she had manners. She would never stick a mustache on a bear she didn't own and then rip it off. She also could speak pig Latin better than anybody I ever met. This Kathleen doesn't begin to compare. *Well, you're not the one we know.*

I give up on holding a conversation with this altogether different Kathleen Casey, while my sister and her new best friend—Kathy she's calling her now—say things like: *Oh, my God. You have to buy this cheese. It is fabulous.*

As the Movember photo shoot wraps up, it occurs to me that there are no clocks or windows here. The Vegas of stores, Costco is a food casino of sorts. It's easy to lose track of time, get swallowed up in the bigness of it all, and pretend that everything is right with the world, that everybody can have a taste if they just line up.

In actuality, it's an exclusionary structure. One must pay an annual membership fee to partake in this elite club that has risen up in a city where some children live in a chronic state of deprivation. It is the 667th Costco sprouting up in a country where eleven million children in kindergarten through twelfth grade live in poverty. Looking around the store, I think of those who are not here, the hungry ones who would love a chance to line up with the unhungry and load their carts up with pumpkin pies as big as steering wheels.

The poor often only get a taste by pressing (without permission) their ravenous bodies into indecorous service. Just the other day, as part of my work with Communities In Schools of Kalamazoo, I visited an elementary school and met several children who have a "disruptive" habit of salvaging leftover lunches from garbage cans. Finding brown bananas and partially eaten sandwiches, they sneak those bits into their pockets to share with siblings who are not yet school-age beneficiaries of free or reduced school lunches. Chronic hunger drives these kids to ingenuity. Living in a low-income neighborhood with no ready access to healthy, fresh, and affordable food, they are hyper-alert, constantly figuring out ways to survive and to feed themselves and their families.

I reach for a beautiful glass jar of roasted peppers and try—unsuccessfully—not to feel guilty as I set it in my cart, imagining how pretty it will look in my stocked pantry. I cross the aisle and end up in a nonfood aisle. I can't quite figure out what this section is all about. Holiday decor? Electronics? I study a long box containing seven cream-colored candles. As I reach for the box, a man brushes up against me and says, *Pimp.*

At least I think he just said pimp. My husband complains that my hearing isn't what it used to be, but I don't know if I believe him. Why would he be announcing he's a pimp? I take in his appearance: shoulder-length hair, a rumpled shirt, and frayed jeans. He's sexy in a stoner kind of way, and I'm currently doubting my ears. *Excuse me?*

These lights, he points to the fake candles on display, *with the fancy remote controls. It reminds me of a movie. From a long time ago. You know what I'm talking about? Oh, who's the guy? That actor? You know, he walks into a room ...*

A lot of actors walk into rooms.

But this guy, he hits a button, and all these lights and music come on.

Dudley Moore? I think he did that in the movie 10.

No. It was a movie made longer ago than that.

At that moment, Kathleen Casey makes another appearance. I almost don't recognize her because her mustache is gone. *I* love *these candles,* she says, pointing to the box I forgot I was holding. *You'll love the convenience of having a remote control.*

Kathleen breezes past us, and I set the box of candles back down.

Stoner guy asks, *Who is the gal who played in those slasher films?*

Jamie Lee Curtis?

That's it. Her dad. What's his name?

I feel like a contestant on a game show. *Tony Curtis.*

That's it. Tony Curtis! Thanks. His voice grows husky. *So, uh, what brings you here?*

Seriously? I think this guy wants to be my Happy Light, and I'm pretty sure he's come to Costco for sex.

I'm here for milk, I lie and skedaddle my lactose-intolerant self out of his presence in search of Holly.

How easily people could have an affair at Costco. It probably happens all the time. A few weeks later, when this thought returns to me, I'll google *Costco* and *love affair.* An hour worth of effort and all I'll turn up is a recording artist named Jeff Costco who started a band called Cheaters and wrote a song called "Ten Cent Love Affair." The band broke up sometime after 1982, so now a bunch of ex-Cheaters roam who knows where. And here's the weirdly ironic part. Jeff Costco starts writing and performing with his wife, Cindy Sams. What are the odds that two people whose last names are the same as the two largest membership warehouse stores in the country are married to each other? Would Walmart, the subsidiary of these two retail giants, put up a fuss if they renamed their duo Costco and Sam's Club?

Right now, I'm on the hunt for Holly. I find her in the frozen food section, laughing with Max, her hairdresser. With dozens of frozen spanakopita in the bottom of his cart, Max waves his hand about the store. *I'm drinking in this event*, he announces.

I look around and try to see the store through his eyes. The place is peppered with faux cocktail parties. There is, admittedly, a festiveness in the air. That's part of the Costco experience. Even though it's opening day, come back any day, and you'll find people mingling around shiny-parked carts, sampling the various wares, and chitchatting with blue-aproned and hair-netted sample hosts. Each host wears a name tag identifying their first name.

As Holly and Max continue to chat in front of a frozen display of a hundred-count Belgian Cream Puffs, Shantaray has quite a crowd gathered around her cart.

Sample anyone?

These blue-aproned sample people like Shantaray are not store employees, but rather, they work for Club Demonstration Services, *the preferred in-house event marketing provider to Costco.* Unfortunately, the sample people who suit up in white shirts, aprons, hair nets, and latex gloves don't receive the same generous benefits that Costco employees enjoy, and they make about twenty percent less an hour even though their efforts make a financial difference.

Offering samples can increase sales, in some cases, as much as two thousand percent. Part of the reason for this, researchers will tell you, is due to the rule of reciprocity. When someone does something nice for you—say, offers you a free sample—you have the urge to reciprocate this good deed and thank them by buying the product you just tried for free.

I'm in love with this place. Holly has saddled up alongside me. *Wanna come back tomorrow?*

I need a break. Maybe in a few weeks. Why don't we check out now? Holly doesn't hear my question since she's taken off again. She's spotted someone she knows.

I look back at Shantaray. An older couple is seriously noshing at her station.

In the Costco world, there are two kinds of people. Samplers and non-samplers. Based on my behavior today, I think I fall somewhere in the middle. Call me a semi-sampler. Since setting foot in the store, I have been offered and accepted samples of flavored water, salsa on a tortilla chip, bitter coffee, salted caramel, a slice of ham, nonfat frozen yogurt, smoked salmon on cracker smeared with Chevre cheese, and another kind of tastier cheese drizzled with balsamic vinegar.

I have also passed by and refused organic orange juice, beef, Shantaray's Belgium cream puffs, cookies of an unknown kind, meatballs, and some kind of smoked meat stick that resembles a hotdog but isn't. I also don't buy the pasta maker that someone is demonstrating.

As Holly stops to talk with the demonstration person, I gravitate back to the non-food aisle. The stoner guy is gone. I pick up the long box of seven flameless pillar candles I'd set down earlier and place it in my cart.

Before today, I never knew I needed them.

Artichoke Dip

Serves 8 to 10

— *2 (14 ounce) cans of artichoke hearts, rinsed, drained, and chopped*
— *1 cup mayonnaise*
— *1 cup mozzarella cheese, shredded*
— *1 cup parmesan, grated or shredded*
— *4 ounce can diced green chilies (optional)*
— *2 teaspoons garlic powder*
— *1 teaspoon cayenne pepper*

1. Heat oven to 350 degrees.
2. Combine all the ingredients and put them in a baking dish or deep-dish pie pan.
3. Bake uncovered for about 25 minutes or until golden and bubbly.
4. Serve hot with your favorite crackers, veggies, or crostini.

Sound Bites

GET IT. IT will change your life. These are the two, terse lines my sister emails from her Verizon Wireless 4G LTE smartphone. I scan the subject heading again. "Costco."

What could possibly be bought at Costco that could change one's life? Vitamins? An automatic defibrillator? I guess it's a good-fitting bra. The wire in the bra I'm wearing has dislodged, and one end is drilling into the base of my left breast. My Maidenform friend has turned on me, daring me to let her go after a decade of togetherness. *Not so fast, girl.* I bunch up some Kleenex and wind it around the end of the drifting wire, tucking it under the bra. The pinching dulled, I click the attached image Holly has included—big boxes stacked on, I presume, Costco shelves. Each box boasts a five-piece set pressure cooker. The sign above reads $59.97.

I don't need to shell out sixty bucks to cook cauliflower in a fancy twelve-gallon thingamabob. The pan I use to steam broccoli, cook rice, or shove under my son's chin when he feels nauseous is good enough for me, thank you very much.

Holly calls the next day and continues where her email left off. *You really need one. They are energy efficient. Prep to serving is under an hour. It's real food. Real good.*

I'm happy for you, but I don't need one.

You do. I bought a cut of meat I wasn't familiar with, a pork blade steak, as a test for my pressure cooker. It came out beautifully. All food comes out beautifully. Oh, my God. I love it. You'd love one.

The pressure cooker people need to hire my sister. Holly could sell pressure cookers like hot cakes to everyone, except me. I tell her this.

Jen, a pressure cooker makes everything amazing. Perfect.

Except when it blows up in your face if you don't release the steam.

That's a huge misconception. Too many safety features now.

I remind her how she kept having to manually release steam last weekend at her potato bar party. What if she had forgotten to do so? Each time she opened the valve, the ambience of the party was marred by what sounded like a woman's high-pitched cry for help. I found it disconcerting, but I admit her other guests seemed unruffled by the occasional screams.

Holly laughs. *I released the steam just to freak you out. I loved watching you jump.*

Yeah, right into the arms of your husband. I almost knocked his drink to the floor twice.

It was the broccoli.

No, he had a drink in his hand, not a stalk of broccoli.

I'm talking about my pressure cooker. The broccoli was in the pressure cooker for the potatoes. I just did a fast release so it wouldn't overcook. You don't need to use much water, so vegetables retain more vitamins and minerals. You really need one. I'm serious.

I know you are.

*

My brother John is a long-distance chorus chiming in. *I can't believe you don't have a pressure cooker.*

It's not until later that I will read that a younger sibling can raise the older sibling's blood pressure by five percent. I'm not surprised and think maybe mine is doubly high, given the pressure coming from both Holly and John. *I have two Crock-Pots,* I keep telling them. *They work fine enough for me.*

Next time I come to Kalamazoo, I'll borrow Holly's pressure cooker and show you the power of what it can do. I'll make brisket. You'll be able to taste the difference.

John hasn't said it, and though he's 744 miles away, I know he is contemplating buying me a pressure cooker for my birthday. I warn him not to buy me one, but then I feel guilty when the excitement in his voice wilts.

But food cooks so quickly. It saves time.

What about savoring time? We live in a world that moves quickly, and for precisely that reason, I try to relish the slow by anchoring myself to the present when cooking. I take pleasure stirring peppers in a pan, watching onions glisten and turn translucent, and hearing oil sizzle and snap. It's easy to adjust for taste along the way. I refuse to turn that pleasure over to a smug, tight-lipped machine.

Later that day, John sends Holly and me a recipe for cooking chicken tikka masala in a pressure cooker. I count twenty-one ingredients. My limit is eight. Ten if I'm fancy. This whole saving time concept is deceptive. The recipe asserts it takes just ten minutes to cook this meal in a pressure cooker. It doesn't account for the time it will take to gather twenty-one ingredients, cut up the chicken, and marinate the chicken for one hour *before* dumping everything into the pot. If I were making this, I'd have to tack on an additional fifteen minutes just to hunt down the garam masala at the back of my cupboard.

Speaking of garam masala, I'm rather pleased with myself, having purchased this Indian spice mix last year for a tasty spinach curry I made. Shoot. I just remembered that garam masala is best used within a few days but can be kept for six months. So, tack on an additional forty minutes to throw out the old garam masala and run to the store to buy fresh garam masala.

That evening, Holly replies. *I just made this* again. *Delish.* She's attached a link to a recipe for pilau rice, made in, you guessed it, a pressure cooker.

I do not share anything.

*

Something is in the water. Even environmentalists are impacted. It's a few weeks later when the president of the Kalamazoo River Cleanup Coalition adjourns the meeting at 8:35 p.m. I'm more tired than I care to admit. I've been a part of this board since its 2007 inception. I've learned that, unlike pressure cookers, justice is not swift. We can't mix together hope, changed habits, and the choicest cleanup solution and expect change in weeks, let alone years. At best, we crawl along at a dog paddle pace. Lately though, it feels like we're treading water, barely keeping our head above the Environmental Protection Agency superfund guidelines and ever-changing deadlines. Decades away from the shores of justice, we wash up monthly to the same old table and catch our breath to sing our discordant song: We must protect our water and restore the eighty miles of river and lands tainted with polychlorinated biphenyls—PCBs. PCBs are bad. They cause cancer and other adverse health effects, so they shouldn't be piled up on or anywhere near our aquifers.

Over the years, we've added new verses to our lamentation, including one for the 2010 Enbridge oil pipeline spill into the Kalamazoo River, one for our Flint neighbors northeast of us who deal with lead-tainted water, and one for the Standing Rock Sioux tribe to our west, who are worried about threats to their water supply.

Tonight is no different, except when the meeting is over and we gather up our coats, hats, and mittens, Bill, a long-time community activist, tells us he just bought a new pressure cooker and loves it. Marla, a biologist and an expert on fish and soil, nods her head vigorously. *They're energy efficient, you know.*

Could there be a parasite embedding itself into brains, causing normally intelligent individuals to spout off about pressure cookers with little or no encouragement?

Did you buy it at Costco, Bill? I ask. Why the hell am I joining in?

No, I ordered it off of QVC. One hundred bucks. He's grinning like he just caught a twenty-five-pound Marlin. *It came with a cookbook and two lids, and you could pick from a range of colors like blue, burgundy, and orange.*

What color did you pick? I hear myself ask. I think it's the writer in me. I am curious.

Eggplant.

Chuck, a neurobiologist and expert in the environmental and health impact of toxic PCBs, saunters over. *I was just about to tell Jen you have a pressure cooker,* says Marla, winding a colorful scarf around her neck.

I love my pressure cooker, says Chuck. *I cook my beans in it.*

He makes unbelievable beans, Marla says.

Chuck … Crap. I'm doing it again. I can't help myself. *Did you use your pressure cooker to make that bean dish you brought to our annual meeting?*

Sure did.

As I recall, that dish was quite tasty. I tell Chuck as much, and he grins.

When I tell them that I don't have a pressure cooker, Bill says, *It makes everything tender and juicy. You should get one.*

As we step out into the chilly, cloudless night, Marla tells us that studies have shown that pressure cookers kill off some kind of toxic fungus that clings to rice.

Driving home, I mentally add rice fungus to my growing list of things to worry about in this world. I also wonder about this pressure cooker hoopla. It's nothing more than a fancy saucepan with a locking lid, right? Perhaps this chatter is just a good way to blow off steam. No pun intended. It's a way to steel ourselves against the barrage of oil spills, climate change, and tainted water that burst from the news each day. The mundane keeps us entertained just enough, so we don't explode with worry.

Later that evening, while brushing my teeth, I start worrying that maybe everybody is right and that I am missing out. At the very least, I should be more open-minded. Before falling asleep, I decide that, come morning, I'll read up on pressure cookers and then make an informed decision.

*

Turns out, pressure cookers aren't that new. We owe their existence to Denis Papin, a French physicist who created its predecessor. Made of glass and metal, it looked like a potbellied stove. In May of 1679, he went with his invention before the Royal Society in London. Composed of intellectual elites of the time—including Isaac Newton—the society served as kind of a clearinghouse for scientific ideas. He described it as *A new digester or engine for softening bones …*

A few years later, a supper was cooked in Papin's invention and served to the fellows of the Royal Society. One of those fellows, John Evelyn, reflected on the meal prepared in Monsieur Papin's digestor and noted in his diary that it was *the most delicious that I had ever seen or tasted. We ate pike and other fish, bones and all, without impediment; but nothing exceeded the pigeons …*

For dinner tonight, pigeon is not on the menu. Instead, I've prepared chicken cordon bleu in a 9 x 13 Pyrex baking dish. I love how the heat from the oven has warmed the kitchen on this cool, fall day. Although my husband and son have second helpings, I doubt either of them will ever write about the experience.

As my boys talk football, I think about Denis Papin. He lived an honorable life, contemplating steam and trying to figure out how he could harness it to move things and to make life better. I feel sorry for this Papin guy though. Today, while you can't throw an apple without hitting a science book with Newton in it, Papin is nowhere to be found.

I interrupt the football conversation to announce Denis Papin invented the pressure cooker. I want my son to know his name. My husband and son each throw out a few comments to pretend they are mildly interested in pressure cookers and Denis Papin. Then, they get back to talking drafts and lineups.

After dinner, I wander into the living room and find a 1689 engraving of Papin in *Encyclopaedia Britannica*. It's in his happier days, and loose curls tumble around his pleasant face and down his shoulders. Most likely, he's wearing a wig that was all the rage during Europe's Baroque era. He has what looks to be—but probably isn't—a white napkin tucked under his chin that fans out over his chest, as if he's ready to dig into a delicious meal he thinks he will be served. Neither feast nor fortune or fame ever comes. He would eventually die a pauper. Buried in an unmarked grave, he's disappeared like steam.

*

Modern pressure cookers cook food seventy times faster than a regular pot. How is this even possible?

The science behind pressure cookers has to do with pressure, force, and area. It's like cooking in heels.

Say the average American woman steps on your foot. She weighs 168.5 pounds and is wearing brown loafers. (I would love a pair of brown loafers.) No, let's go with the average Bangladeshi woman who weighs ninety-five pounds. She's stepping on your foot. It hurts a little, right? Now imagine that this same woman leaves the room and returns wearing high heels. Same woman stepping on your foot, but this time the pressure is concentrated in a smaller area, into the pointy heel part. It hurts a lot more. It would be less painful to have her step on your foot with brown loafers than crunch down on it in high heels.

I've always equated heels with danger, so no wonder my body submits to its fight-or-flight response under the onslaught of pressure cookers, aka high heels. As a prepubescent girl, I tumbled down some stairs while wearing church shoes with chunky, one-inch heels. As my body lay at the bottom landing, the heel of the right shoe lay halfway up the stairs, and the heelless shoe blazed dozens of tiny nails into my buttocks. High heels equal a pressure cooker. That adds up to danger.

Manufacturers and food bloggers attempt to assuage our fears, telling us that this is not our grandmother's pressure cooker and that the exploding horror stories we may have heard about are urban legend. This cooker is safe to use, and numerous safeguards have been incorporated.

Safe things though, like pencils and my hand-me-down cooking pot, don't require safety features. Nuclear power plants, guns, and pressure cookers have safety features.

It's probably safe, yes, *if* used according to manufacturer's instructions. But the world is spinning a thousand miles an hour, and most of us don't bother to read or heed the fine print. Even if we do, safety features can fail. Google *pressure cooker mishaps,* and your screen blows up with five hundred and seventy-seven thousand stories of burnt breasts, damaged vision, and the severing of an elderly woman's leg. Best case calamity: fill the pot a tad too much, the vents clog, and you're eating baked beans off the ceiling.

Hold on. There's even a law firm specializing in pressure cooker explosions. My hunch is there is no lawyer out there representing people who cook with plain pots. I can't prove it, though, since searching *lawyers* and *pots* only turns up firms providing cannabis and hemp-related matters.

*

Researchers have discovered that younger siblings take on more risks than their older brothers and sisters. In a study of seven hundred brothers who played major league baseball, the younger brothers were ten times more likely to steal bases than their older brothers.

This tendency must, I assume, apply to cooking behavior too. It would explain why my younger siblings get a thrill from pursuing this culinary shortcut and fervently promote the use of a potentially explosive pressure cooker. Holly and John need to stop pressuring me to cook like they do.

My idea of risk-taking is making overnight apple pie steel cut oatmeal. I prepared it only once as the experience was too stressful. I put oats, apples, cinnamon, vanilla, and several other ingredients in a CorningWare dish. And this is where the daring part comes in: I placed the covered dish *inside* my slow cooker. Yes, inside. Then I carefully poured in water until it was one inch below the top of the dish. I put the crock's lid on and set it to low. I went to bed, and for a restless eight hours, I kept waking up, worrying that it had been unwise to stick a dish inside the Crock-Pot. I got up once, thinking I heard a suspicious crackling sound coming from the kitchen. I snatched my reading glasses from the bedside table, thinking they might shield my eyes from flying ceramic shards. My heart pounded as I entered the kitchen. All was quiet. Only cinnamon swirled.

*

We're coming to get you, Holly informs me, having just picked up our mother to spend the morning shopping and then going out to lunch. This is the first I'm hearing of this plan.

When I turn down her invitation to drive one hour to Dowagiac, population 5,740, and shop at some ladies' boutique I've never heard of, she sighs loudly.

I remind her it's Friday, my writing day.

They have high-waist pants, Holly says, trying to woo me. *You know how hard it is to find high-waisted pants these days?*

It's. My. Writing. Day.

So? she says.

So, I want to write.

Whatever, she says and hangs up.

I write for four, gloriously uninterrupted hours. The silence is shattered by my phone ringing. It's Holly. *Come outside. Mom and I are here. In your driveway. We want to show you what we bought.*

I look down. I'm barefoot and still in pajamas. *Why don't you guys come inside for a minute?*

No, you come outside. It's your writing day, and we don't want to bother you.

Holly's reasoning seems logical enough. *Okay,* I say and hang up the phone.

I see your nips, Holly says.

It's cold, and I didn't have much time to dress for the occasion. I hug myself to keep from shivering as they showcase their Dowagiac collection, pulling pants and shirts from plastic bags one at a time, asking me to guess what they paid for them, and telling me before I can toss out a guess. I wonder if any neighbors are watching this fashion show unfold in the driveway.

As my sister holds up the climactic piece—a stunning, smoke-colored dress—my mother sizes me up from the passenger's seat, leans over Holly, and shouts, *I hope to the good Lord that you'll change before your son comes home from school. You don't let him see you like that, do you? I could not stand myself if I looked like that.*

Thanks, Mom.

Holly leans out the window, grinning, her phone poised to shoot. *I'm going to snap your picture.*

No pictures! I shout, turning away from them and running back inside.

I sit down in front of the computer, hoping to salvage the remaining minutes of my writing day. I scrape a silver maple leaf off the bottom of my foot and deposit it in my empty coffee cup. I stare at the blinking cursor. Eventually, I type, *I see your nips.*

*

Later that evening, perhaps as a peace offering or maybe because she is relentless, Holly sends me a link to a post titled "Why I Gave Up My Slow Cooker for the Instant Pot." After studying the photo plunked at the beginning of the piece, I don't care to read why Elizabeth Barbone has shunned her slow cooker. I'm already turned off by the Instant Pot that threatens to lull my common sense asleep with its shiny look and eighteen buttons. Yes, eighteen. I counted them. And what's with the "Porridge" button? Are people seriously making porridge these days? The last time I came across porridge was in a nursery rhyme. I can't even spot an "On/Off" button. Ms. Barbone is not selling me on the Instant Pot. Holly could give her some pointers.

As an on-and-off-switch kind of gal (although I delight in the occasional dimmer switch), I want to know who is taking it upon themselves to buttonize our world and call it progress. It doesn't take long to find out.

Screw you, Robert Wang and your button-loving friends at Double Insights Inc. It's rather cheeky of you to market this jumble of choices as *unparalleled simplicity*. Your Instant Pot website proclaims, *We are now in the era of smart cookers*. Oh, you are good. I see what you did. You've replaced *pressure*—a word that naturally creates a feeling of, well, pressure—and inserted *smart*. Who doesn't like smart? And isn't instant what we're all after? Instant results whether it's success, weight loss, or a homecooked meal? The era of working hard for something and putting one's own time and energy into it is passé.

As meteoric pots pelt the culinary landscape, I feel like a dinged-up dinosaur. How much longer can I survive this onslaught of pressured sound bites?

Get this. The company blames their button problem on their customers. It seems their pot has become a gateway to craving even more buttons on pots. Running out of room on the pot itself, they now push designer Bluetooth pots that can be remotely controlled with mobile phones. *The most intriguing fact*, the website notes, *is that any user can program the "iPot" with an intuitive graphic interface, without worrying about the cooker blowing up.*

As a hardcore landliner and one of the five percent of Americans who doesn't have a cell phone, I find this all confusing. First of all, it's not an intriguing fact to point out that something won't blow up. What kind of fact is that? Also, in their buttoned-up Insta-world, we are no longer people who cook but users who program.

I imagine myself embracing the cold future of now, in which I've evolved from dinosaur to avid pot user, the Bluetooth kind. I see myself executing Goat Curry in a Hurry, compiling the ingredients outlined in the food blog, *My Heart Beets*. I shove the hind quarters of a goat into the pot and run into the living room. Hunkered behind the couch, I pull out my phone and push "Sauté."

After the meat has browned—how will I know if it's browned?—I guess my phone will tell me—I return to the kitchen and add in garlic, onion, ginger, turmeric, and my stale garam masala. I need to stir-fry this for three minutes, but I don't see the "Stir Fry" button. Instead of panicking, I press the "Plus" and "Minus" buttons a few times and run out of the room. I return minutes later, dump in potatoes, water, and tomatoes. Securing the lid, I close the pressure valve and loop back to the safety of the couch. The goat is supposed to cook on high pressure for forty-five minutes, but I can't find the proper button. It is not intuitive.

Fortunately, I notice I'm wearing brown loafers. My breath steadies. I improvise and depress "Meat/Stew" on my phone. After forty-five minutes of waiting, I am worn out and too afraid to check on this instant meal, which isn't instant after all. I hate programming. My husband finds me behind the couch, crying for the days of dull pans and dim-witted slow cookers. He kisses the programmer, and we instantly forego the Goat Curry in a Hurry.

Stew on that, Instant Pot.

Pigeon-Free Chicken Cordon Bleu Bake

Serves 8-12

Unless serving a crowd, put one (unbaked) in the freezer for another time. If you're looking to stretch this meal, serve over a bed of egg noodles or rice.

— *8 cups cooked chicken, cubed*
— *4 cups cooked ham, cubed*
— *1 can cream of chicken soup*
— *¼ cup milk*
— *8-9 slices swiss cheese*
— *3 cups shredded cheddar cheese*
— *2 tablespoons Kick'n Chicken Seasoning*
— *12 ounces (2 boxes) stuffing mix*

1. Preheat the oven to 350 degrees.
2. Spray two 9 x 13 pans with non-stick cooking spray.
3. Mix milk and cream of chicken soup together. Set aside.
4. Prepare stuffing according to directions on the box. Set aside.
5. Toss the chicken with Kick'n Chicken. (My brother turned me on to this seasoning. If you can't find it in a

store near you, just substitute 1 tablespoon paprika, some garlic powder, onion powder, and a dash of red pepper flakes.) Equally distribute the seasoned chicken in the two pans.

6. Layer these ingredients in the following order: ham, swiss cheese, and 1 ½ cups of the cheddar cheese, soup mixture, stuffing, and remaining cheddar cheese.

7. Cover and bake for 30 minutes.

8. Uncover and bake for an additional 10 to 15 minutes.

What I Wanted to Say

When you returned my Sunday call
left with your answering service and I told you
her pulse was erratic, blood pressure fluctuating wildly
and reminded you of her diagnosis of atrial fibrillation,
what I wanted to say was
her heart cannot hold another. I have only known
my mother's heart to be big enough to hold the sky.
To think of it as only one fluttery muscle in this vast world
frightens me.

When you asked of other symptoms and I told you she
        was dizzy,
I should have told you that our world is spinning, that my
sister has driven across town and dragged a vacuum cleaner,
mop, and other cleaning supplies into my parent's
perfectly clean home because she wants to do something,
it is the only way she knows to be of some assistance
as she is a comet burning, streaking across the living room
with her swiffer, saying *I just love this Swiffer, especially*
with the long handle attachment. Do you have one?
I don't know how I ever managed to dust before

this invention, and I couldn't find the long handle of mine, so I'm
so glad I found yours. Mom, do you mind?
My mother puts one hand to her head, the other hand
waves away this noisome child.
When did my mother's hands grow old?

I wanted to mention that between beats my mother
worries that her husband isn't going to have a proper
dinner. When she creaks out,
Oh, honey. I wanted to fix you that beautiful roast you
        bought the other day,
my sister stops with the swiffering and says,
        I'll fix the roast, and flies
into the kitchen, and we all—my mother, father, sister, and
me—breathe a sigh of relief that she could now safely
orbit a chunk of meat.

When you asked about her dosage and I told you
it was twenty-five milligrams of Rythmol,
what I wanted to say was my father seems suddenly old
and helpless, his hands shaking as he tries to comfort
his wife with pillows, food, and pills, all of which
        she is refusing.
She is swatting us away like gnats, but we can't help
        but hover near her.
We are drawn to her. She is our light.

Because it happened after we got off the phone,
I couldn't report this to you
but my sister, in the middle of preparing the roast,
stopped and demanded of my mother—*Who did you call*
first? I live closer and you should have called me. Why didn't you
call me? —my mother sighed, *Your sister called me.*
This immediately appeased my sister who
gravitated back to seasoning the roast.

When you paused, I heard myself fill the silence, saying,
        She just isn't herself.
What I was trying to get across is that she is the type
of woman who likes to be in control, who takes pride
in not asking anything of others. Her phone rings steadily
throughout the day with friends and acquaintances calling to
get her advice or get her take on their ailments.
So, when she called and asked, *Can you come over?* I said,
Sure, and hung up the phone, leaving the dryer's mouth
        opened wide in amazement,
clothes tumbling over themselves and spilling onto
the floor.
        Running out the door,
I found her in the shower unable to step out.
I toweled her off like she did for me when I was little.
I helped her dress and watched her watching me as if
somehow I could make her better.
So, you've got to make her all better please.

Fix her fix her fix her.
Then my sister can stop dusting,
my father can stop wringing his hands,
and I can be her daughter again.

When we hung up, I don't think you heard me at all.

Slow Cooker Roast

Serves 6

— 3 to 5-pound beef chuck or round roast (Select the size that will fit in your crock and allow room for the ingredients below)
— 1 small bag baby carrots
— 5 potatoes, quartered (I use what I have on hand, usually russets)
— 5 yellow or white onions, quartered
— 7 garlic cloves (or more)
— 3 teaspoons garlic powder
— ¼ cup water
— 1 packet onion soup mix

1. Scatter several of the onion quarters on bottom of crock and then set the roast in the pot.
2. Dust some garlic powder over the roast.
3. Put remaining onions, carrots, potatoes, and garlic in the pot.
4. Add water.
5. Sprinkle soup packet over the ingredients.
6. Place the lid on slow cooker and cook on low for 8 hours or until roast is done.

Kissing the World Goodbye

BASH IS DEAD.

It is hard to gauge my sister's level of emotion over the phone. It sounds like she is sipping coffee and crunching on something hard—a carrot, maybe—when she tells me this. So, while my heart wants to tread lightly, my mouth has a mind of its own, as is often the way when it comes to my sister.

Who the hell is Bash? I inquire.

Bash is a part of this family, she says, as if that explains it all.

I don't say anything because ever since earlier this week when my coworker ran out of the office to be at her husband's side, I'm paranoid that maybe I suffer from periodic transient ischemic attacks (TIAs), in which the blood flow to parts of my brain stops for brief periods of time. That would explain a lot. Like how I sometimes feel strange for no good reason at all or how my memory is developing an incommodious habit of abandoning me to go on long walks with time or my keys.

For my colleague's husband, this type of forgetting is an unusual occurrence and cause for concern. Following his regular workout regime, he can't recall his routine of cool-down stretches, his locker combination, or the name of the painter who has meticulously been painting their kitchen a mossy green for three weeks now and is like part of the family. These are small things, the doctor tells my colleague and her husband, but it is a warning. A sign that something bigger, like a stroke, could be looming on the horizon.

I bandy the name about my brain. Bash, Bash, Bash. Did we once have an Uncle Bash? Is one of my second cousin's kids nicknamed Bash? Maybe Bash is the last name of a childhood friend. A teacher named Bash whom we called Mr. B? This intimate stranger lurking in the shadows makes me uneasy.

Hello? Are you there? I said our fish just died.

I should be relieved but annoyance slips in. *Bash is one of the fish you got yesterday?*

Yessss. I can tell *dumb ass* is flicking on the end of her tongue by the way she hisses the *s* in *yes.*

You named the fish? Already? Hearing the note of disapproval in my voice, I hope she hears it too.

We named all *the fish,* she replies defiantly.

You shouldn't name your fish, I chide. *For at least a week.* My made-up-on-the-spot wisdom goes unheard as she rattles on about the new water plant she bought.

I am worried about my nephew, King. How can Holly not be worried about how this death—tiny though it may be—will affect her son? How quickly does it take for a child to bond to a fish anyway? A month? A few days? Less than twenty-four hours? Naming something—even a fish—extends power to the relationship, tightening the bond between namer and named. So, when something bad happens to the named, the namer—in this case, my nephew—may suffer more than if a nameless fish simply ceased to be. My sister should know this. She named her son King, and he rules her life now.

Listen, I tell her. *I have to let you go. I've got to get Tom to school and head into work.*

You'll let me *go? I hate it when you say that. I think I'll let* you *go.* And she does.

*

Communities In Schools. This is Jennifer. May I help you?

His wife kicked him out of the house. Holly's voice. It's been two hours since she hung up on me. Apparently, I've been forgiven for attempting to let her go. I hold my breath and dive into the darkness of memories lost, looking for snatches of conversations in which Holly has confided about a friend's troubled marriage and come up empty-handed. Maybe I am suffering from TIAs, or maybe it's something bigger. Perhaps the horizon is here.

I give up, Hol. Who are you talking about?

Phil. You know, the guy we bought the fish tank from?

The guy you just met the other day?

She mistakes the credulity in my voice for concern. *Don't worry,* she soothes. *It happened years ago. And all because he had too many tanks in the house. Can you believe that? Phil said that his wife told him either she went or the tanks went. Isn't that wonderful? If it wasn't for his wife, we wouldn't have this great pet store in town. He was so helpful. Really, just a beautiful person. And just so knowledgeable about fish. Did I tell you about what he said about the cycles?*

You did. Yesterday.

And did I tell you how I bought live bacteria and put it in the fish tank because otherwise the fish will all die? Phil calls it New Tank Syndrome.

Yes, that too. You called the other night and the night before that, ecstatic with your purchase of live bacteria and meeting some guy—apparently Phil—who said it would help with New Tank Syndrome.

It's incredible to think that fish poop turns into ammonia. It builds up and up. Phil refers to it as a nitrate spike. You have to pay attention to the tank cycle. Put the fish in at the wrong time, and the fish die.

I didn't think fish were that complicated.

Me neither. But it is worth all the trouble. The fish just mesmerize King. I can't peel him away from the tank. Remember watching the fish poop when we were little? I loved that. I could watch them poop for hours.

You are sick, I tell her, and we both laugh.

Do you want to come over and see the fish tank?

No, I'm doing a little something I like to call working. Maybe later this week. I should get back to work now.

You should get a fish tank, she says.

I don't want one.

Why not? Suspicion rises in her voice.

I just don't.

Well, you should get one. Think of your son and how much he would like it.

I start typing quietly. *Listen, I'm going to let you …*

What? she says sharply. *You're going to let me go now? Oh, how nice of you.*

No, I'm going to let myself hang up the phone. But Holly has already hung up on me.

Bye, I say to nobody.

*

Later that afternoon, when I'm home, I call Holly. Tom, my seven-year-old son, has just finished his homework and is lounging on the family room couch, strumming on his guitar and watching *Dog with a Blog.* I'm making a flourless chocolate torte and need to know if I can substitute the dark rum that the recipe calls for with the light rum that I have on hand. Before I can ask, she says with a hint of pride in her voice, *We watched him die.*

You watched him die? I say, pulling a sack of flour down from the pantry shelf. Its papery lips emit puffs of powdery dust, indignant that I hadn't closed it properly during its last use.

Yes, Holly replies. *King and I both watched him die.*

I assume she is referring to Bash, and I simultaneously imagine the scenario if the fish had died in our home. My husband would make an excuse to go into his office, I would write a poem and title it "Demise of Bash," and Tom would slink off to his room, pick up his guitar, and write a song titled "I Watched My Fish Die."

121

Creating is the best way I have learned to adapt to both the big and little woes of this world. I have passed this trait on to my son.

My sister, however, hurtles through the world, latching on to sundry things—be it a hobby or a notion—embraces it vehemently, and then, without fanfare, lets go and moves on. At this moment, neither Holly nor I could predict that in the coming months she, a connoisseur of wine—who has pooh-poohed my porters and amber ales over countless glasses of wine—will take up beer brewing.

We will argue repeatedly over whether or not she even likes beer. I will swear to it that I've never seen her put a beer to her lips, and she will swear that, in my selfishness, I have failed to notice her deep appreciation for the foamy beverage. Our phone calls will revolve around how she and her husband invested in a Bell's deluxe beer brewing kit. However, she will not be able to wait for the freshly purchased ingredients to ferment in a six and a half gallon ale pail.

She will research exercise machines and purchase a top-of-the-line stair stepper, only to call later, yeast still rising, to inform me that she is fatter than ever. For now, though, she is five pounds lighter, and our focus is fish.

I worry that King, who is wrapping up his third year of life, does not have an outlet to deal with fish death properly. What if an I-watched-my-first-ever-favorite-fish-die tape runs often, wearing away at his precious mind and carving out rivers of sadness until he is worn away? *You're not planning to add more fish for a while, are you?*

You mean besides Dash and the others? I don't know. Maybe. What the hell is it to you?

Dash? Others? *Who is Dash?*

Bash's brother. Or sister. She laughs.

This isn't funny, Holly. Don't add any more fish. At least for a while, I warn. *I really have to go,* I say, but not before invoking Phil's name, reminding her about his nitrate spikes and New Tank Syndrome warnings. I hang up, having forgotten to ask Holly about substituting light rum for dark. I call her back.

Light rum should be fine, she says.

Thanks, I say, already pulling down the rum. *Love you.*

Love you, too. We hang up in unison.

I pour the torte mixture into the springform pan and place it in the oven. I open the freezer door and, as cold air licks my face, contemplate supper. I pull out a package of tilapia, the crystallized filets pressed together like thin white lips. It seems disrespectful to serve fish for dinner in light of Bash's recent demise, so I stuff the tilapia back in the freezer and decide to make vegetable stir-fry. I put a pot of rice on the stove and cover it with water.

I can't stop thinking about Bash. My mind reels in his final moments: his tiny body bloating, floating up, then dangling over the toilet bowl, an insignificant splash as Holly's fingers release him, translucent scales swirling 'round and 'round until he disappears. I call Holly back. *What did you do with him?*

Do what with whom?

Bash. I squeeze the phone between my shoulder and my ear and start chopping an onion.

He's on the kitchen counter.

Oh, my God. I cease cutting the onion. I envision King sitting on the kitchen counter stool, finishing his breakfast as his small brown eyes are drawn to Bash's lifeless body splayed out next to a bowl of Raisin Bran.

Maybe you shouldn't keep a dead fish on your kitchen counter.

Oh, Bash is fine.

He's dead, I remind her. I resume cutting the onion.

He's in a bucket.

Who's dead? It's Tom. I hadn't heard him enter the kitchen.

No one, honey. Don't worry about it.

He continues to stand there, brow furrowed.

What's the matter? Holly says on the end of the phone.

Seriously, Tom. Everything is fine. Go back and watch TV.

I have to go to the bathroom.

Then go to the bathroom. He hesitates and then heads out of the room.

Why didn't you flush him down the toilet? I whisper into the phone. *Why a bucket?*

That way, Ted can see Bash when he comes home from work.

Fine, whatever, I sigh. It's not worth arguing.

We hang up, and I begin separating a head of broccoli by hand. I recall a study that researched the relationship between fish watching and memory. People diagnosed with Alzheimer's improved their memory through fish watching.

There was this other study too that said just having a fish—or maybe it was a pet in general—increased the survival rate of heart attack victims. Something like one year after suffering their attack, ninety-four percent of fish owners were alive compared to only seventy-two percent of those who were fishless.

I don't think I'm making this up, and I don't think it's a coincidence that there is, throughout this country, an epidemic of aquariums bubbling away in doctor's offices. Healthcare workers must know that aquariums allay people's anxiety before a tooth is yanked or a horrible diagnosis is pronounced. With the horizon fast approaching, the fish bring some small amount of peace.

It occurs to me that the Department of Motor Vehicles should consider adopting this aquarium practice. Stepping into the DMV is an anxiety-inducing situation. It is not a natural thing to do—to take a number and wait—forced to sit in an uncomfortable chair, along with an assortment of your fellow citizens who are also sitting in uncomfortable chairs, many of them looking like they shouldn't be on the road at all, let alone driving a bike with training wheels.

As you wait for your number to be called, there is much time to worry. About all the drivers on the road and how a shocking number of them are missing one or more of their front teeth. About your child who will, too soon, be sharing the road with them. About how judgmental you really are. You worry that you will be late to your next appointment when the woman two numbers smaller than you decides that it is suddenly a good idea to start yelling at the glassy-eyed DMV clerk about how she pays enough taxes and the government shouldn't make her pay to renew her license. Yes, fish could help.

By now, I'm hoping the negative side effects that King may have experienced due to the premature death of his finned friend have been cancelled out by the positive effects of fish watching. This thought provides some solace. I just wish Holly shielded King a bit more. I know she thinks I should shield less with my parenting. She's probably right.

Just the other evening while I was reading aloud to Tom at bedtime, I caught myself censoring Harry Potter's friend Ron Weasley. J.K. Rowling has written this character with quite a mouth on him. Twice, I automatically changed his *damn* to *darn*. I probably tend to err on the side of caution, but buffering any child from one less *damn* in this life is perhaps an honorable thing to do. At least that is what I tell myself.

I look down at the cutting board and realize that while I was thinking about memory and parenting styles, I have thoughtlessly felled an entire forest. Tiny trees of toppled broccoli populate the cutting board, their slaughtered stalks spilling onto the cool granite.

*

I wish I could enjoy my slice of chocolate torte as much as my husband and son savor theirs, but with every warm bite melting in my mouth, I think of coral reefs, the rainforests of the seas. An article I'd read recently said that climate change, as well as the depletion of coastal shorelines, is killing off these underwater *trees* at an alarming rate. They will slip from this world, the author cautioned, and then we will not be far behind. *The horizon*, the article cautioned repeatedly, *is here.* Everything we do—no matter how small it seems—matters.

We are, whether we are aware of it or not, connected to everything.

*

I'm rinsing a plate when the phone rings.

I wish you had a chance to know Bash. You would have loved him. He shimmered like the sun. He was beautiful. We loved him. Holly's phone eulogy lasts longer than the life of Bash.

You've been drinking, I say, starting the dishwasher.

So what? I bet you have too.

You got me there. Two glasses of wine. What about you? I drag a damp cloth across the counter.

One. Holly starts laughing. *Bottle of wine, that is.*

I wait until she stops laughing. *So, what about the other fish?* I venture. *Did you name them too?*

Ferdinand. He's a Red Molly. Diesel 10. Gordon—he's the blue Mickey Mouse platy. And then, of course, the Rumi-nose tetras, Dash and Bash.

Holly granted her son's wish to name all the fish. And King, who is in the great train stage of life, has chosen to bestow names of his favorite Thomas & Friends characters upon the fish.

A crash is coming, a crash is coming, a voice chugs in my head. I don't know whose voice it is, but it sounds suspiciously like my mother's, taking on the same tone as when she says, *Heaven help us.* If my sister continues speeding along this track, taking her son along for the ride, New Tank Syndrome or Nitrate Spikes could loosen the couplings. Everything could become unhinged.

You there? You want me to take Tom with us?

Sorry. Just thinking about King and his love of trains. What were you saying?

Tomorrow I'm taking King to Phil's place, letting him pick out a fish in honor of his fourth birthday coming up. Want me to pick up Tom after school? He can come with us, pick out a fish, and name it too.

I don't want my son picking out a fish that will probably be dead the next time he visits it. But I say, *I don't see the point in Tom picking out a fish that hangs out at your house. He'll hardly ever see it.*

Get your own tank then. Or maybe you'll just have to visit me more often.

Don't you think you should slow down with this fish buying?

Screw you. I'll buy as many fish as I want. Anyways, we have live bacteria to combat the New Tank Syndrome. Listen, I really want you to check out the fish tank. Will you come over tomorrow night? Have supper with us? I'll make homemade pizza. I've got a fabulous crust recipe I want to try out, and I'll make up a whole bunch of toppings that we can slather on it.

Sounds good. Okay. I'll bring something. Maybe beer.

No, just come.

*

Lighting up the dim hallway is a rectangular patch of water encased in glass. It's a watery monument, a shimmering shrine of love to her King. Fish, like jewels, flash sapphire and ruby bodies, winking in and out of dark green plants bought from Phil.

King runs to my side, presses his nose against the glass. *That's Dash*, he explains. *He's a Rumi-nose tetra.* My eyes ignore the flickering fish passing by and follow his finger pointing to a tiny translucent green torpedo lodged at the base of the tank. Tetra should sport a crimson nose. Dash's is a dull pink, which bleeds out around the eye and into a thin line that races across the length of his body.

Dash is not living up to his name. He hovers at the bottom of the tank, his sliver of a belly grazing the colored gravel. This fish, I realize, is dying, following in the footsteps—or rather finsteps—of his brother or sister, Bash. Both Rumi-nose tetras. I wonder if this breed of fish is named after the great prophet Rumi.

King extends his arms, hugs the tank, and peers eye to eye with his dying companion, his soon-to-be second loss of the week. What is my nephew thinking?

It is almost easier to figure out what is going on inside the fish. I take Dash's stillness as an awareness that the horizon is here. As he peers out of his watery tomb, a calm defiance settles in. He seems to echo Rumi's own words in knowing that his own death was near: *How doest thou know what sort of king I have within me as companion? Do not cast thy glance upon thy golden face, for I have iron legs ...*[1]

The fish and the boy contemplate each other. King, who is first to avert his eyes, says with bravado, *His brother Bash is dead.* He then runs down the hall, yelling, *Tom? Where are you, cousin Tom?*

The surface of the water quivers. Dash's one black eye, a period made with what looks to be the tiniest of pens, does not look away.

*

Born in 1207, Rumi grew up in what is now known as Afghanistan. A wise and prolific poet, this Muslim mystic is wildly popular today, at least by Barnes & Noble's standards. The bookstore closest to where I live is stationed along South Westnedge Avenue in Kalamazoo. It devotes an appallingly huge selection to his works within the paltry section set aside for poetry.

I can't help thinking it would bother Rumi, a peaceful man who valued diversity, to know that his words were taking up so much space, squeezing out the prophets of today. Rumi believed that poetry, as well as music and dance, lead to God. If Rumi had beheld this swirling dervish of fins and fronds within Holly's tank, it's not hard to imagine he would have pronounced fish watching a path too.

---

[1] Nasr, Seyyed Hossein. 1987. *Islamic Art and Spirituality.* New York: State University of New York Press.

Rumi-nose tetras may be the prophets of the fish world, the first to divine impending trouble. Do fish heed the prophetic voices of their own kind, or do they, like people, ignore the voice that calls out to them more often than not?

Dash is dying, I say, saddling up to a stool at the kitchen counter.

Holly shrugs. She is, I realize, already moving on.

As a pan of slivered onions caramelize on top of the stove, Holly expertly stirs mushrooms. The aroma is divine.

Don't you think it's odd, I ask, *that the Rumis are the first to die?* When she doesn't respond, I say, *Maybe Rumi-nose tetras are more sensitive than other types of fish. Kind of like a canary in the coal mine of the water world.*

Dash is a rummy-*nose, not Rumi-nose*, she corrects me. With hands encased in oversized mitts, she pulls her lightly cooked pizza dough out of the oven. She tosses the mitts onto the counter and starts smearing a homemade marinara sauce over a golden crust.

I thought you said it was a Rumi?

No, it's a rummy. She sounds almost bored.

So, this tropical, freshwater fish is *not* named after the prophetic voice of Rumi after all. It is a *rummy*-nose tetra. As in the two-player card game Gin Rummy. Rummy is a world of winners and losers: five is better than three, a king is greater than a queen, and aces are considered deadwood, something to be readily discarded. This misnomer saddens me.

I slide off the stool. Holly proceeds to slice the red peppers she roasted earlier in the day. I amble back to the fish tank.

Dash's fin is ready to fold.

I stare at the tank, hoping to inspire calm. Instead, a memory surfaces. My long-dead grandpa sits in a folding chair across the card table from my not-so-long-ago-dead uncle. Both have one of their hands wrapped around a glass of something that, when you try to smell it, burns your eyes and nose. Ice cubes jangle. With a glint in his watery eyes, my uncle snaps down cards, declaring, *Gin!* My grandfather picks up a pencil, and on the small pad of paper that sits at the corner, he neatly keeps score.

*

Pizza is ready! Holly yells. It is hard for her to wait for everyone to trickle in from the living room, the bathroom, or, in my case, the dark hallway.

Time to pray! Before we have fully formed our circle or had a chance to grab hold of the hands on either side of us, she bellows, *Bless us, oh, Lord, and these, thy gifts ...* Other voices join in; my sister softens.

In that sliver of a moment, while we remain coupled and have yet to release each other from ourselves, I silently call upon the Rumis of this world, using some of the poet's own words from a favorite poem of mine, "A Great Wagon." *Thank you for tending a square patch of world where all are welcome and there are hundreds of ways to kneel and kiss the ground.*

Chocolate Raspberry Torte

Serves 12

Over time, my flourless chocolate torte recipe morphed into a dark chocolate (and still flourless) raspberry torte. No rum required! If you want a bigger contrast between the layers, simply substitute white chocolate for the semi-sweet chocolate chips.

— *6 eggs*
— *1 cup butter*
— *16 ounces of dark chocolate (I use Ghirardelli Chocolate Extra Bittersweet 70% Cacao Baking Bars)*
— *1 cup semi-sweet chocolate chips*
— *8 ounces of whipping cream*
— *1 package (8 ounces) of cream cheese*
— *1/3 cup powdered sugar, plus more to dust*
— *½ cup seedless raspberry jam*
— *Fresh raspberries*

1. Preheat oven to 400 degrees.
2. Melt the butter and the dark chocolate in a heavy saucepan. Stir until smooth before setting aside to cool.
3. In bowl, beat eggs for 5 minutes on high speed. This will pump up their volume nicely.

4. When the chocolate mixture has cooled, gently fold in the eggs and pour into a 9-inch springform pan that has been sprayed with nonstick cooking spray.

5. Bake for 15 to 20 minutes. The center will jiggle a bit, but the edges of the cake will be set.

6. Cool on a wire rack for about 1 ½ hours and then refrigerate until firm, which is another 1 ½ hours.

7. Heat semi-sweet chocolate and 3 tablespoons of whipping cream in a heavy small saucepan over low heat. Stir frequently until the chocolate is melted.

8. In a large bowl, beat cream cheese and powdered sugar. When smooth, add this to the chocolate mixture, continuing to stir until smooth.

9. In another bowl, beat the remaining whipping cream until stiff peaks form. Fold into the chocolate mixture. Spread it with the spatula over the cake.

10. Refrigerate until firm, which is at least 1 hour.

11. Prior to serving, heat raspberry jam in a saucepan on stove.

12. Lightly dust torte with some powdered sugar.

13. Using a spoon, place a dollop of the heated jam on each dessert plate. Smear with the back of spoon to give it a whooshy look. Set the torte slice in center of the plate, scatter a few raspberries on and besides the torte, and serve.

Time Traveling on Creston Street

When a smaller box s is situated, relatively at rest, inside the hollow space of a larger box S, then the hollow space of s is a part of the hollow space of S, and the same space*, which contains both of them, belongs to each of the boxes. When s is in motion with respect to S, however, the concept is less simple …*

— Albert Einstein, *Relativity and the Problem of Space*

HONEST TO GOD, tiny tumbleweeds of dust, cat hair, and dog hair roll across our feet. The real estate agent's mouth is moving, but his words are garbled in the musty air. My sister and I travel room to room, where unfinished or poorly executed projects loom. Here and there, walls are slashed open. We avert our eyes, trying not to notice the exposed insulation. Fuzzy pink tongues hang out in surprise.

I step onto the sunporch that melts into a screened porch that hardens into a walled patio, where, in the middle of this open house, I stagger over my younger self sunbathing with the neighborhood cat, Clarence, who's dozing on my back. My sister disappears, but not before handing me a sledgehammer. My father arrives, and, side by side, we rage against the concrete walls. My father, in his white T-shirt that's translucent from his sweat, causes the house to tremble. Tomorrow and three houses later, he'll stumble while playing golf, fall at the ninth hole, and hurt his knee. He'll refuse ice.

Oh, here's my sister, curled on the couch sleeping. She's nestled next to our grandpa, who's smoking a pipe and watching the Detroit Tigers. Our brother has just flown in from Spain and is playing with blocks. We're all falling asleep. The risk of falling into melancholy mounts until my mother, wearing a fashionable wig and looking like Mary Tyler Moore, runs down the stairs. Instead of singing, *Love is all around, no need to waste it*, she's screaming lyrics not quite so catchy, like *damn it, I'm nobody's maid. I wish I had become a nun and never given birth to you.* For the chorus, she throws clothes, shoes, a hairbrush, books, and a box of Girl Scout cookies—Thin Mints—out the front door. This doesn't stop people from piling in; these people that can't see we are always dusting here on Creston Street.

Our dead Chihuahua dashes across the room, my brother not far behind. *This house is one hot mess*, a woman says, eyeing me as she heads downstairs, where period underpants soak in a bloody pail. Somewhere, a floorboard moans.

Now we're emptying plaid beanbag ashtrays that float away to eBay. We clean bathroom mirrors each week until they squeak while some other ghost of a family flecks the mirrors with dried spit and toothpaste.

Open the linen closet, and they're all there: the same endless exchanges wafting through the house. The sweet, syrupy voice of Jean Nate whispers into Dorothy Hamill's Short & Sassy Shampoo. The green, no-nonsense bottle of Phisoderm is off by himself while the too-piney Clairol Herbal Essence claws at the Tussy deodorant.

Folding in and out of itself like a bellowing accordion, the fabric of time is pleated. I'm ten years older than my mother, who is shaving her legs in the bathtub. I open the Emeraude, the cheap little bottle that dared to live on after my

136

grandmother's heart stopped beating. My grandmother rushes from her grave. Flush with death, she puts on a Tom Jones record. *My, my, my Delilah …*

We dance past my mother, who never became a nun and always bore us up. She's wearing an apron now, Bermuda shorts, and no wig because she's tossed the wig, along with her walker, into the air. She's stirring Hamburger Helper on the stove, my sister at her side. We are all so happy: my mother without her walker, her undead mother, my sister, and me. We could all be friends.

Slush from the Seventies

Yields a lot

This is a recipe passed down from my mother's friend, Carol. When we lived on Creston Street, my mother always had a big vat of slush on hand for parties and unexpected guests. She kept it in the basement freezer, and it was my job to lug it up and down the stairs.

— *1 large 7-up (2 liter)*
— *A fifth of vodka (whole bottle)*
— *1 can of orange juice (12 ounces)*
— *1 large cranberry juice cocktail (62 fluid ounces)*

1. Mix all the ingredients together in a large container with a lid.
2. Seal the lid and place the container in the freezer. In the process of freezing, take it out and stir a few times.
3. When it's time for a book club, a picnic, or a family reunion, pull it out, stir it a bit, and scoop into tumblers.

Butter Love

I DISCOVER MY sister's latest hobby while in line at Bilbo's Pizza. While standing behind my son's former first grade teacher, Mrs. Haulenbeek, I tap her shoulder.

Oh, my goodness, Mrs. Haulenbeek says, turning around. I expect her to inquire about Tom and rave how much she adored teaching him. *Your sister's butter is divine!*

We love her butter, her husband chimes in. As they go on about Holly's butter, I vaguely recall that she babysat their boys years ago.

The next day at work, my colleague, who is Facebook friends with Holly, asks, *Do you know when Holly's next butter run is? I'm almost out.*

A week later, in the fiction section of the Kalamazoo Public Library, the wife of my son's soccer coach approaches me. *Where does your sister get it?* she whispers.

The butter? I correctly guess. I don't tell her where she gets it because I don't know. Being Holly's sister, you'd think I'd be privy to her butter dealings. But just like how she won't tell me the whereabouts of her secret Up North family cabin, she's also shrouding this facet of her life from me. She probably has an irrational fear that I'll elbow in on her butter market.

From what I can piece together, my sister's foray into butter entails periodically driving somewhere to obtain vast quantities of butter that she then cuts up, packages, and sells to old boyfriends, Facebook pals, mothers of boys she once babysat, and others who enter her orbit. Holly is on a holy quest, using Facebook to reach the masses and offer up heavenly butter that, according to her butter believers, has saved their cakes and humble toast and inspired them to be better cooks. Her butter has made them brave. They try new brownie recipes and toss in ingredients they've never used before into their soufflés. Holly, in her own way, is saving the world one buttery brick at a time.

Even though she hasn't clued me in on her new venture, I'm proud of her. She's created demand where none had been months earlier. I need to know more, so when my mother phones at the end of my workday and says, *Your sister just stopped by, so why don't you swing over and join us for Happy Hour?* I do.

*

When I arrive at my parents' house, my father is in his favorite position: reclined in his chair with his hands clasped over his belly, gazing at nothing in particular. I hear my mother and sister in the kitchen opening and closing cabinet doors, the sound of ice cubes plinking into a glass.

Penny for your thoughts. I love asking this of my father. In all the years I've asked, his responses are never *nothing* or anything as mundane as *the weather.* Even though his thoughts often involve invertebrates, he's never failed to surprise me.

In order for scientists to understand the major errors infecting current evolutionary theory, I'm thinking I need to write another blog post. Condense some key thoughts into one post. I've talked with you about pogonophora, the previously unknown link in the evolutionary sequence that connects annelid worms to vertebrates, haven't I?

Like a hundred times.

I guess that's right, he chuckles. *Well, I should probably get to it. Can I get you a glass of wine before I do?*

That would be lovely. Thanks.

A few minutes later, my sister and I, curled up on each end of the couch, sip red wine as our mother sits in her recliner, nipping at her Manhattan cocktail. My father, tucked away in the computer room while working on his pogonophora post, misses the rundown on the fabulous sale going on at Talbots. With butter on my mind, I'm not joining in the conversation because I'm too busy listening for a place to jump in. I finally interrupt.

What is this whole butter thing about, Hol? Why haven't you told me that you're selling butter now?

You need to get with the twenty-first century and get on Facebook. Then you'd know.

I launch into my I-shouldn't-have-to-sign-up-for-Facebook-in-order-to-learn-what-is-going-on-in-the-lives-of-my-loved-one's speech.

Holly laughs.

My mother lifts her Manhattan to her lips. Ice cubes titter. *Did Holly tell you about that famous author contacting her? How she is going to follow Holly around on one of her butter runs?*

What? No! What's the author's name?

Oh, I forget her name, Holly says with a dismissive wave.

It will be a feel good story about your sister and her butter.

It's nothing definite yet.

You didn't agree to it, did you? Sign anything?

I told her sure, whatever. Holly takes a sip of her wine. *What do you care anyway?*

I care because you're my sister. And if anybody should write about you and butter, it's me. I sound whiney and immature, but I can't stop. *I didn't even know you were doing butter until last week. But if you had told me, I would have gone with you.*

Like I said, Jen. Get. On. Facebook. Holly sips her wine, looking quite pleased with herself.

Facebook won't tell me what butter means to my sister. That's what I want to understand.

*

For thousands of years, butter has enjoyed a holy status. Krishna, the Hindu god of love, is terribly fond of butter. In Hindu literature, stories abound of this divine thief stealing butter from everywhere, digging his hands into the pilfered pots and sharing the finds with his friends. In one poem, the sixteenth-century poet Surdas depicts Krishna as a baby god crawling on his knees, his face smeared with butter and framed with curls that bounce *like swarms of bees*. He holds fresh butter in his hands. In many poems and stories, he isn't hoarding the butter or keeping only the best for himself. Nor is he sacrificing his share. God and friends alike partake in the joy of eating butter. There is enough for all to be satisfied. No one needs to go without.

Krishna and his relationship with butter hints as to how ancient Hindus understood the nature of the divine. Playful and childlike, Krishna reminds us that butter—one of many

142

treasures in this world—isn't meant to be locked away but shared with abandon, for the good of all. When we equitably distribute the butter, we also feed ourselves. Maybe this is what Surdas is getting at in his poem where, crawling along, baby Krishna encounters a polished pillar and offers butter to his shining reflection.

Both Krishna and Holly seem to operate from a similar vantage point. Holly with her Hindu heart passes out butter for the pure fun of it. She has no hidden agenda. For her, butter is friendship and love, and she is simply passing this along. Without realizing it, Holly is playing out this divine theme of love, manifest in butter.

*

I try again. *So, Mom, do you know where Holly gets the butter?*

I'll be back in a minute, girls. I have to get dinner in the oven for your father. Macaroni and cheese tonight. I've already made it. Just need to pop it in the oven.

I watch my mother slowly make her way to the kitchen. Maybe I'm paranoid, but I think she's avoiding my question. In fact, she's probably already gone on a butter run with Holly. I glance over at my sister who is fingering through a *People* magazine. *So, where do you get the butter?*

Without looking up, and in rather un-Krishna-like behavior, she flashes me a middle finger.

I'm serious, Hol. I need to know.

Like everybody else, you can read about it in the article you're not writing, she chuckles, then laughs harder when the bird she has just flipped at me flies back at her.

I'm not a jealous person, but this butter talk makes me bitter. *How about you let me go on a run with you first?*

She asked first.

But I'm your sister.

Sorry. She doesn't sound sorry.

We sit in silence for several minutes. That's when I notice a large cardboard box in the corner of the room. *What's with the box?*

It had butter in it, shrugs Holly. *It's gone now.*

Why she has dragged an empty butter box into our parents' home, I don't know. *None for me?*

I didn't know you wanted any.

I didn't know you were selling the damn butter.

Language, girls, my mother says, returning from the kitchen.

Sorry. Hey, if I had known, I would have bought pounds and pounds of it. That's a lie, but I want to make Holly feel badly for excluding me.

I've got some in my fridge at home for folks who have ordered it. If they don't pick it up, you can buy it off me. Three dollars a pound.

A Hindu god is less of a mystery than my sister. I just want to understand this butter business so I can fathom her more fully. If Holly won't help, then I will steal my way to enlightenment. It seems easier and less of a hassle than opening a Facebook account and placing an order for butter.

I eye Holly's precious butter box and quietly fish my car keys from my purse. When Holly brings the wine glass to her lips, I make my move.

144

Bye, mom, I say, running across the room and snatching the empty box. I'm already out the door and down the porch steps when it registers with Holly what I've done.

Come back here with that box! she yells, racing after me. Her shouts jangle the quiet of Bronson Woods retirement community.

It's just a box! I retort, not looking back.

It's my fucking box!

It is her box. And I'm stealing it. What am I doing? My crummy knees wonder too, complaining vigorously that we do as Holly says and stop, but I assuage my guilt with this thought: *Krishna stole butter.* Almost to my car, I'm laughing like a crazy god, drunk on the thought of butter. Though Holly, with her longer, three-years-younger legs, could easily overtake me, I've caught her off guard and achieved enough of a head start to make it to my Subaru Forester. Opening the car door and flinging the box into the passenger seat, I jump in the car, slam the door, and start the engine. Unlike Krishna, I am only a stealer of empty butter boxes.

As I make my getaway out of Bronson Woods, Holly stands in the driveway with her hands on her hips, screaming, *Go ahead, keep the damn box! But no details! Do you hear me? No details!*

*

I pull into the garage, turn off the car, and set the box on my lap. My index finger traces the black-inked words. Helvetica Bold font, perhaps? I love getting lost in the details, and Holly knows it. My sister's worry is my hope—that I will find her somewhere in the details.

The box is brown, indiscreet, and modest. Made in South Bend, Indiana. My thoughts wander to the people who make these boxes. I imagine their open, honest faces smiling back at me. Do they feel fulfilled creating something that will not outlast them? Do they ever wonder about the people who open the boxes they make?

This box once held fifty-five pounds of creamery butter. *Fifty-five pounds!* I exclaim aloud, to nobody. The butter, if the box is to be believed, is all real. Two percent salted. This butter should be refrigerated at forty degrees or less. Or freeze at zero degrees or less.

I get out of the car and swing the box onto my hip. A part of me wants to let Holly know I haven't heeded her "no details" demand. I could call her up and whisper, *Sub lot no. 010-036,* and then hang up the phone. That would really piss her off. Laughing like a lesser god of butterless boxes and noticing no further details, I break down the cardboard booty and toss it into the recycling bin.

*

Butter, according to the great State of Wisconsin, is *made by gathering the fat of fresh or ripened milk or cream into a mass, which also contains a small portion of the other milk constituents, with or without salt or added coloring, and contains not less than 80% milk fat.* Wisconsin, America's Dairyland as their license plates remind you, forbids the substitution of margarine in lieu of butter in any public eating place (unless ordered by the customer). Everyone, Wisconsin preaches, deserves butter, even prisoners.

Violate one of the oleomargarine regulations set forth by the Wisconsin State Legislature and you may be fined one hundred to five hundred dollars and imprisoned up to three months. The good news is that you'd get butter on your bread in jail.

As the second largest butter-producing state in the nation, I realize Wisconsin law is grounded in economic reasons, but it resonates on a deeper, spiritual level. Everyone deserves butter, and you don't have to be good to get it.

Maybe it's menopause poking, but I almost weep at this thought: Everyone deserves butter.

*

A history lesson on butter that I never learned in school but wish I had:

First, there were dinosaurs. Then wooly mammoths, followed by shaggy yaks, which gave way to yak butter tea. During the Iron Age, the Irish buried barrels of butter in bogs, the cool peat preserving lumps still churning up today.

Butter, *chemah* in Hebrew, slipped into the Bible and transformed into hospitality. Sarah and Abraham served boiled calf and buttered bread to strangers. After offering to wash their feet, Abraham stood under the shade of a tree and watched the three angels eat.

In time, those in power learned to wield butter as a weapon. The enslaved were often bathed and rubbed in shea butter to shine and sell, as if a person could be plucked and presented like polished fruit. For Sally Carder, enslaved in Oklahoma, the only chance to taste butter was when it was waved under her nose. When a misdemeanor was done, she said, *My mistress would give a buttered biscuit to the one who could tell her [who] had done it.*

On the other stick, acts of defiance have been waged against a backdrop of butter.

Some years back, a butter churn discovered in South Carolina cracked open the life of a slave named Dave.

Born about 1801, he was a potter and poet. Day after day, he'd throw raw clay on the potter's wheel, creating beautiful, balanced vessels for his owners. Around the opening of one of his butter churns, he carefully wrote this couplet into damp clay: *This is a noble churn / fill it up it will never turn.* He signed it *Dave* and dated it. According to him, on yet another vessel, he wrote, *Dave belongs to Mr Miles / wher the oven bakes & the pot biles.* That one was dated July 31, 1840.

Keep in mind, he was doing this in a time when reading and writing, let alone composing couplets, was a crime for those enslaved. Save for several years, he fired his cursive words onto wares that wagoned worlds beyond where he could go. Utilitarian containers of the day, his pieces held all sorts of items, from butter to meat to shoes. On one, dated May 13, 1859, he wrote, *Great & noble jar / hold sheep goat and bear.*

The enslaved, no doubt, would be loading and unloading the heavy pots from the wagons, reaching into the richness of Dave's work and pulling out the meat for their masters, butter for their mistresses, or food for the slaves. Hovering below the lips of one of these pots, Dave's words were, *I wonder where is all my relation / Friendship to all—and every nation.* It was written August 16, 1857.

Might his own relations, sold like butter, have pressed their fingers against the green and yellow glaze, tracing a Black man's words that hovered right under the white glaze?

On June 28, 1854, his owner, Lewis Miles, criticized one of his handles. Dave, though lodged in the shadow of slavery, wrote neatly on the jug, *Lm says this handle will crack.*

The handle, to this day, holds.

*

I feel bad for cows. Those doe-eyed animals are the backbone of American butter, trying to keep up with the average American's annual intake of twenty-three sticks of butter per year. That's almost six pounds. It takes twenty-one pounds of cow's milk to produce one pound of butter.

Though Holly's butter box was made in Indiana, most likely she's making butter runs somewhere in Michigan. Which of Michigan's four hundred and three thousand cows contributed to her butter? I want to meet this cow and stare into her big, brown eyes.

The next day, I'm still thinking about cows when the doorbell rings. It's Holly. Arms stretched, she holds out two blocks of butter wrapped in parchment and tied with red and white twine. She has already forgiven—or forgotten—that I stole her box. *I thought you might want to try some*, she says. *You don't have to pay me.*

I invite her in for coffee. *Can't*, she says. *Have more butter runs to do.*

I accept her offering. *Do you make the packages this pretty for everybody?*

It's the most practical way to do it. Keeps the butter fresh, plus you can store it in your freezer like this.

Are you figuring in the cost of parchment, ribbon, twine, your time, and your travel with what you are charging for the butter?

Uh, no. Her tone suggests she's just been asked the most ridiculous question in the history of butter transactions.

It's a bad business model, Hol. It's not sustainable. People love the butter, and I'm sure they'd be willing to pay an additional fifty cents or whatever that number turns out to be when you incorporate your expenses.

That's not the point, she shrugs. *I love this butter, and I want everyone to have it. Love ya,* she says, heading back to her car, but not before tossing me a beautiful smile.

Holly's approach to allocating the world's resources goes against conventional practice that suggests we slather the riches on ourselves. As L'Oréal tells us, *you're worth it.* We don't live in a pamper-the-poor world bombarded by commercials encouraging us to indulge the poor because *they're* worth it. In my sister's world, everyone is worth her love and time.

Krishna and Holly, in their Butter Love, have much in common. Like Krishna, Holly's behaviors suggest that the wealth of this world is meant to be shared. It doesn't matter who has done the hard work of churning and packaging the butter, the fat of the milk belongs to all.

My love doesn't feel as pure and holy. I dole mine out more carefully. Less concentrated and watered down, it's more diffuse and has sometimes contained questionable properties. Mine is a Margarine Love.

*

We have the French chemist Hippolyte Mège-Mouriès to thank for inventing margarine. Upon improving a medicine used for syphilis, he ventured into more appetizing research areas like bread-making. When Napoleon III, looking for a less costly substitute to feed his army and make available for his people, offered a prize for a butter substitute, Mège-Mouriès mixed beef fat with milk and salt and won the award in 1870 for his invention, oleomargarine. *Oleum* means oil in Latin, and *margarites* means pearl in Greek, describing the pearly drops formed from the oily animal fat extract.

Today, margarine must contain at least eighty percent fat to label itself margarine. Any product containing less than eighty percent is called a spread.

*

Unlike my sister, cows probably hold grudges. I put one butter block in the freezer and the other in the fridge. I wonder if a grudge-holding cow contributed to this condiment. Has anybody done a study to find out if a cow's bad attitude mars butter? It must on some level. Cortisol, a human stress hormone, has been found in human breast milk, and at high levels it can mess with babies' behavior, causing them to be irritated, fearful, and angry. Wouldn't the same hold true for cows? I recall Holly's butter customers that I've run into recently. They don't seem irritated or stressed. In fact, just the opposite: glowing and relaxed. This butter is definitely the product of a grudgeless cow.

*

I take comfort knowing that, not just sisters, but entire nations have battled over butter.

Margarine arrived on the shores of America in 1873 and quickly gained traction. It was affordable and available, particularly to those living on the margins. Wholesome butter, once taken for granted, seemed in need of defending. The butter people—the dairy industry—got scared and started smearing the reputation of the new kid on their golden block. *Margarine linked to insanity!* Anything short of butter was portrayed as an abomination, anti-American.

States started churning out laws prohibiting the manufacture, production, and sale of margarine. Congress soon got busy protecting butter, and seventeen years after the birth of oleomargarine and seven years after its inventor Mège-Mouriès died destitute, President Grover Cleveland signed into law the Oleomargarine Act of 1866: an act defining butter and imposing a tax upon and regulating the manufacture, sale, importation, and exportation of oleomargarine.

In 1931, with the butter battle still raging, Congress had another bill before it. This one was to amend the 1886 law by increasing the tax on colored margarine and reducing the tax on un-colored margarine.

John Nelson, a member of the U.S. House of Representatives from the Great Dairy State of Wisconsin, took to the floor to share his concerns of margarine masquerading as butter. *They can sell oleomargarine until hell freezes over if they sell it as oleomargarine at one-fourth percent tax.* This sentiment was met with applause. Mr. Nelson continued. *We do not interfere with them at all, but we say, 'You shall not by fraud or stealth usurp the trade-mark of butter, its yellow hue.'*

He then launched into the history of margarine, noting that from its onset, margarine was a menace and *the dairy interests clamored for protection for its life at the doors of Congress.* He shared comments from his concerned constituents that margarine had become too powerful ... *The attack has all but begun. No corner of the state is too remote for its presence, no table so humble, no dining room so grand, no lumber camp so rough, that oleomargarine, with its mellow name, will not walk upon and into, with a deceitful bow and brazen smile, with the claim that its name is butter.*

Congress concurred, and the amended Oleomargarine Act remained in effect until 1950.

In 1959, Eleanor Roosevelt, who had a soft spot for the marginalized and downtrodden, rallied to margarine's side and did a commercial for Good Luck Margarine. Thomas Stix, her agent at the time, recalled her reasoning behind doing the commercial. *With the amount of money I am to be paid, I can save over six thousand lives. I don't value my dignity that highly.*

Sitting at a table with toast and a bone china teacup, the former First Lady of the United States looks directly into the camera. *Years ago, most people never dreamed of eating margarine. But times have changed. That's what I've spread on my toast—Good Luck. I thoroughly enjoy it.*

Less than a decade later and three years apart, my sister and I were born. Margarine was savoring its heyday. If my sister and I could be considered average Americans, according to the United States Department of Agriculture, Holly and I were devouring twelve pounds of margarine a year, compared to—if we had been around in 1958—8.9 pounds by 1972.

*

I'd take greater delight in preparing tonight's meal of macaroni and cheese if I hadn't stumbled over this fact: an estimated fifty-one percent of all workers on dairy farms are immigrants. This means butter is built on the shoulders of our most vulnerable. That knowledge rattles my insides, realizing these people can't stop to eat the butter because they have long days of dirty, hard work. They get up before dawn, care for cows, clean up manure, and do whatever it is they do so they can get paid low wages while I consume the fruits of their labor.

With elbow macaroni boiling in a pot on the stove, I pull Holly's butter out of the fridge. Who cared for the cows who made this butter possible, and what are their stories? I cut off a slab to add in with the cheese, slicing away until it looks like I have half a stick. Several soft shards splinter off, reminding me of Dave the Potter.

Dave, who later took the last name of Drake, put in long hours to turn out over an estimated forty thousand pots from his owners' kilns. He signed his name, leaving traces of himself for archaeologists to find. He knew the words he scored into the skin of his pots, along with his handles, would live beyond his last breath. Despite his confinement, he found a way to both endure and bust through his enslavement, and even time, his lines still reaching out to us, traveling through space. *I saw a leppard, & a lions face / then I felt the need of — Grace* (November 3, 1858).

Dinner is ready! Serving up mac and cheese with a side of peas, I say a silent prayer of thanks for Dave, dairy farmers, and the multitudes of nameless people behind butter and its many vessels.

The three of us, gathered around the dining room table, dig into this meal made with butter we don't deserve. Thank

God, for grace. As Tom and John talk Western Michigan University basketball, I feel full-on Butter Love for them and study their familiar faces, knowing this moment is fleeting. There have been families before us, assembled in this very space. One day, another family will navigate these rooms and take our place.

Stop staring at me, mom.

Sorry, Tom. In the blink of a cow's eyes, our life will be over. What will we have to show for it? Fragments, possibly, our work unearthed like Dave's, some of it reassembled into a patchy past, our names scrawled on paper, pots, or, if we're lucky, in the lives of those we leave behind.

Hey guys, you might be interested to know that I've been reading the Congressional Record from 1931. The Senate is battling over butter and oleomargarine and using words we never hear anymore, like hither and thither. I continue my monologue for a few more minutes, weaving in a few facts I've learned from scanning through a study conducted for the National Milk Producers Federation.

That's great, mom. I'm going to my room to do homework now. I watch my son cross the room and disappear down the hallway.

At least my husband, a political science professor, will be impressed. I expect John will momentarily lean over the table, kiss me hard on the lips, and say, *My God, I married the perfect woman!* The next day, he'll brag to his colleagues about his wife and her dazzling insights into the 1931 butter debate of the third session of the seventy-first Congress.

With his plate empty, John stands. *You know a lot about butter that nobody cares about.*

But you must!

No, he shrugs, *not really. I've got papers to grade.* He carries his empty dinner plate to the kitchen.

If my husband doesn't care to hear about my margarine musings, then I will reach out to someone who does.

*

Dear Mr. Balmer,

I've been thinking about butter lately. As CEO of the American Butter Institute, you probably think a lot about butter too.

If butter is a religion, then I'd say I'd lost my way until the 2008 Bob incident. I almost don't want to tell you about this as you'll conclude I'm a crappy daughter-in-law. But I want to be real as butter, so here's my story.

It was a Monday morning, and my in-laws, Bob and Mary, who are two of the most generous and loving people walking the planet, were sitting at my kitchen counter. I'd made them a pancake breakfast before they headed home to Indiana.

I left the room for only a minute. Upon returning, I couldn't believe it. "Bob!" I screamed. "What are you doing?"

They both looked up like startled deer. Bob had unscrewed the top of our I Can't Believe It's Not Butter! spray and dumped the contents on his plate. A puddle, the color of melted canaries, cascaded down his pancakes.

"It was just coming out in squirts," he explained.

"That's the whole point!" I shouted. "I can't believe this!" Nor could I believe I was yelling at Bob about I Can't Believe It's Not

Butter! Thankfully, my husband had already left for work, and my son was at school. I took a deep breath, and in a shaky but quieter voice, I said, "The recommended dosage is four squirts." The bottle, now empty, should have lasted for months, even if we went crazy with five squirts.

"You have to understand," Mary said, recovering and cutting into her syrup-only pancakes. "Bob grew up on a farm eating real butter slathered on real corn that he'd plucked only minutes earlier from the field. Why, when we first were married, I quickly learned to cook ..."

As she spoke, I shuddered at my stinginess, having chosen a plastic bottle of watered-down contents with a hint *of butter over the richer and truer thing. Didn't they deserve real butter? Didn't my entire family? Didn't I?*

This shameful scenario could have been avoided if I hadn't allowed myself to be influenced by the I Can't Believe It's Not Butter! advertising campaign. They sure toyed with the American public by having Fabio, the Italian hunk with the chiseled jawline and flowing blond hair, as their fake butter spokesperson. It's only now, in writing to you, that I see their slick advertising worked on me. That realization is like a goose in the face.

That's what happened to Fabio, you know? I don't remember the details since it was over twenty years ago when he was helping publicize the inaugural run of some fancy, new rollercoaster. He and his blond mane were sailing through the skies of Busch Gardens when his face collided with and killed a Canada Goose. At least I think it was Canadian. The photo was all over the news, so you probably saw it too. As the roller coaster concluded its run, Fabio was in the front cart. His windswept hair unharmed, but he was in a daze and his face was splattered with blood.

Blood makes me think about how your butter people made margarine people dye their product pink to make it look less appetizing. A little harsh, don't you think? Those margarine people were just trying to make their way in the world. No wonder when you required them to sell it in its natural state of grayish white, they sold it with pellets containing yellow dye that could be kneaded into the oleo. Tricky, eh? Though neither of you appear to pull these kinds of stunts anymore, butter consumption in the US is nearing a fifty-year high. Everyone is seemingly content to let margarine be margarine or whatever it is calling itself these days.

Please be assured that margarine, spreads, and fake butter sprays haven't been inside my refrigerator since that day I yelled at my father-in-law.

Yours in butter,
Jennifer Clark

P.S. I have some butter questions. When you get a moment, could you please respond to them. See attached.

Attachment: Twelve Butter Questions

I've been dreaming about cows lately. What does that mean?

The ungulates never speak. Except last week, one nudged her shaggy blue head against my bedpost as if it were a gate. Her eyes, two soft pools of bruises, spilled over me. *It's not the butter; it's the breath,* they seemed to say.

Can Krishna put on the body of a cow?

Is my sister a secret weapon of the butter industry?

According to the obituary of The Butter Cow Lady, Norma "Duffy" Lyon, *her life-size butter sculptures of cows, Elvis, and even Jesus and his disciples delighted Iowa state fairgoers for nearly half a century.* Any chance you have one of her busts on display at the American Butter Institute?

Do you believe that Barack Obama won the 2007 Iowa caucuses because The Butter Cow Lady carved a twenty-three-pound butter bust of him?

How much influence does butter have in this country?

Do you think of margarine as less than?

If you had a sister and she lived in Southwest Michigan, where would she go if she wanted to purchase fifty-five pounds of creamery butter?

Does butter represent love, justice, hospitality, or something else entirely? Right now, I'm leaning toward love because I suspect butter is the concentrated form my sister's love now takes.

In America, forty percent of butter is consumed between Thanksgiving and New Year's Day. Is that because we're all just trying to harness love? (I don't think I will ever be able to harness my sister's love.)

If you were to grade the flavor of my love, would it be sharp? Salty? (Know that the color of my love is barky brown.)

Chefs say lobsters and crayfish produce the brightest butter. My father says crustaceans have an exoskeleton that they must first shed for growth to occur. What must I shed to move forward?

*

I don't mail the letter. It seems like I'm looking for absolution for not loving butter and others as well as I could. But it wasn't a waste of time to write, as I gained insight into the perils of advertising. Plus, I've started to consider my own slippery history with this most delicious condiment.

*

My relationship with butter traces back to the 1970s when margarine was king, and those Blue Bonnet sticks that *bake like butter for less than half the price* were always in our fridge. After all, *Everything's better with Blue Bonnet on it!* My sister and I were pampering ourselves with Love's Baby Soft, pulling our long, dark hair back with Goody Twin Bead Ponytail Holders, and shaking a Magic 8-Ball to find out if the boys we loved loved us back.

Coming home from Saint Monica's Elementary School, we'd immediately shed our plaid uniforms, jumped into jeans or corduroys, and watched ABC Afterschool Specials that often featured adorable boys like Lance Kerwin. Oh, my God. I had a major crush on him and the way his smooth blond hair covered his ears. I was twelve when he played James in the television show *James at 15*. Whatever happened to him?

I'm on it like Blue Bonnet! Wikipedia says my childhood crush gave up acting to become a minister. In 2010, he and his wife *pled guilty to falsifying documents to obtain state medical assistance and to recruiting minors for deviant behavior in Hawaii*. He served five years of probation and now sells time-shares for a resort. Glad I never hooked up with him.

But back to butter. My sister and I were coming of age when you could eat a pat of Imperial margarine and—da-da-

da-da!—a crown appeared on your head. At least that was the way it worked in the commercials. Snap on the television and pro-margarine messages regaled us that fake butter was the way to go. One commercial especially comes to mind.

With daisies wreathed around her head, Mother Nature sat on a rocking chair in the middle of nature and ate what she mistakenly thought was butter. *It's too sweet, too creamy* to be anything but butter, she said. When the voice-over person told her, *it's not butter*, she rose. *It's not nice to fool Mother Nature*, she admonished, causing peals of thunder and lightning that frightened the forest creatures. A raccoon covered its eyes, and the camera cut to a soft tub of fake butter sitting on a log, looking perfectly natural. Not rattled at all by Mother Nature's outburst, the jingle singer crooned to a smooth tune, *You may think it's butter, but it's not … It's Chiffon.*

It was good enough to fool Mother Nature, but that was forty years ago, and Mother Nature can only be fooled for so long. Butter is back in, and let's be honest, Mother Nature isn't in as good as shape as she was then. In fact, at this moment, Dena Dietrich, the Pittsburgh-born actress who played Mother Nature, is currently residing in the Motion Picture Country Home in Los Angeles.

I start loading the dishwasher and realize pro-margarine messages must have melted into my mother's subconscious too. She did all the grocery shopping and the cooking. Unless we were visiting my grandparents, we never ingested—that I can recall—anything other than margarine. When it came time for dinner, we'd plop buttery spreads like Country Crock in the middle of the table.

I dry my hands on the kitchen towel, pick up the phone, and dial. *Mom, do you remember those butter ads from the 1970s?*

My Lord, no! I was busy giving birth to your brother, and after that, I was back at work, grading papers and raising you kids. I was too busy to sit down and watch television. I don't remember anything from that time, let alone commercials.

*

My sister and I sit on her back porch, drinking in trees and late afternoon breeze.

I take a sip of the habanero margarita she has made for me. *This is really good, Hol.*

Not as good as John's. Our brother makes the best margaritas. She takes a healthy swig of her drink. *I wish he was here with us right now. If I could blink him over from North Carolina, I would. Wouldn't that be great? Hey, did I tell you what happened the other day when I was grocery shopping?* She then launches into a story about being in line behind some strange lady, paying for her groceries, and driving her home.

You could have been killed.

I wasn't.

It could have been a setup for all you knew.

It wasn't. She needed help, Jen. She was in a bad way. You would have done the same thing.

Doubtful. My sister slathers her love on everyone who crosses her path. As a practitioner of radical, indiscriminate love, she doesn't wait to find out if they are worthy. She simply unleashes her love on them and me. I will never tell her this, but I want to be more like her: to love unbridled and without fear.

She smiles at me, and I smile too. I'm dangerously on the verge of understanding her. But then, she all but abandons butter.

She's into chickens now.

Macaroni & Cheese with Butter, Please

Serves 8

This recipe can easily be doubled to feed a crowd.

— *1 pound elbow macaroni*
— *¼ cup (½ stick) butter*
— *3 cups sharp cheddar cheese*
— *1 cup Vermont white sharp cheddar*
— *2 ounces cream cheese*
— *½ cup milk*
— *1 can (12 ounces) evaporated milk*
— *½ teaspoon black pepper*
— *1 teaspoon garlic powder*

1. Grease inside of the crock with some butter. Do not use margarine. Turn the crock on high.
2. Add the butter and the cheese into the crock. (If preferred, 1 cup Velveeta cheese can be used in place of the Vermont cheddar and cream cheese.)
3. Cook macaroni to be firm.
4. Drain the macaroni and add to crock. Stir.
5. Add both milks, pepper, and garlic powder.
6. Stir and then place the lid on crock. Turn the crock to low and cook for 2 ½ to 3 hours.

Fourth Grade Place Settings

LUNCHTIME IS OUT of hand, children, Sister Josephine shouts, stabbing a fork in the air. *You have made a mockery of this school and wasted precious money ruining these forks. This childish behavior will stop immediately.*

The only thing that seems out of hand is our principal, Sister Josephine, all red-faced, piercing nothing but air with a droopy-looking fork. I realize, for the first time, nuns have breasts. Each time Sister breathes in, Jesus, on his shiny cross, rises. She exhales, and he falls. *Nuns are the brides of Christ,* Sister Josephine once told us. So, Sister is married to Jesus, and he is always with her, rising and falling with the tremendous tide of her bosom.

I wonder what it feels like to be Sister Josephine's husband, surfing on the edge of her world, arms outstretched, and rising over a sea of startled faces as a hot wind of wife rushes down his spine. I feel badly for Jesus. He is a good husband, always there for her and riding her every breath. He must be tired of her yelling. It's too bad she seems to have forgotten him. If Sister Josephine hadn't leashed him to her neck, he could break free and sit at our lunch table. I'd offer Jesus a bite of carrot along with half my peanut butter and honey sandwich, and he could put an arm around Danny Fremont, who is crying, and tell Danny not to be afraid of his roaring wife. Jesus rises.

Then falls.

The next day, we eat lunch, gaping at the cafeteria's bulletin board. Peace has disappeared, the cardboard flowers and doves replaced with mangled utensils. Whoever did this was determined. It must have taken great effort to wire silverware to corkboard.

Sister Josephine marches past my table and I feel myself shrinking. Sister's husband looks even smaller today, just a shiny, trembling crumb of man. *This is what you have done,* snaps Sister Josephine, standing before the gallery of forks, tines curled in disgust. Her chest is a churning storm, and Jesus is drowning. *I hope you are pleased with yourselves. The next child I catch bending our silverware—*

It never occurred to me that I might possess the power to bend metal. Holding a spoon between the table and my stomach, I press into it. Sister Josephine drones on.

My spoon thrusts back its shiny head and laughs.

Spoon Bending Noodles

Serves 8

This recipe easily doubles, and leftovers make a fun hot or cold lunch. In fact, it's so delicious either way that your utensil might bend in delight. I made up this recipe years ago when I needed a quick dish for a potluck picnic. It was a huge hit, and I've been making it ever since, though it has morphed over the years. I've recently started adding harissa paste to give it an added kick. (I get this Tunisian chili pepper paste from Trader Joe's.) It can be omitted if you want a less spicy dish.

— *1 pound (16 ounces) thin spaghetti*
— *6 or 7 scallions, julienned*
— *4 garlic cloves, minced*
— *1 tablespoon fresh ginger, grated*
— *5 tablespoons soy sauce*
— *1 tablespoon oil (sesame or canola)*
— *1 tablespoon harissa paste*
— *2 tablespoons sesame seeds, toasted*

1. Cook spaghetti to be firm, according to package instructions.
2. While pasta cooks, lightly toast sesame seeds in some butter, stirring often so they don't burn. Set aside.

3. When the pasta is cooked, drain in a colander and put in a large bowl. Toss noodles with harissa paste.

4. Whisk together the soy sauce and oil and then toss the mixture in with the noodles.

5. Add scallions, garlic, and ginger. Toss again.

6. Sprinkle in sesame seeds and serve. Or, if you plan to serve it later, store it in the refrigerator in a sealed container and serve cold.

A few closing words about alewives

I ASK MY father about alewives. He leans forward in his chair and tugs on his lap blanket. He's always cold these days.

I testified on alewives at a state congressional hearing, you know.

No, I didn't know. What did you say?

I advised that alewives had value and that they weren't the total disaster people were making them out to be. They were outcompeting perch, he explains, so salmon were introduced to eat the alewives. Tired from talking, he closes his eyes. It isn't spring, but he's already moving downstream. I can follow him only so far.

It's been a good run, he says. *I'm ready. Though, I would like to see my son. One last time.*

And he will. He'll hover in brackish waters, take two deep breaths, and then head out to sea.

Peas on Toast

Serves 4

When I asked my mom what my dad's favorite dish was, she said, *Food*. Thinking further on it, she said, *Toast*. My father did love a good, and even bad, piece of toast. My mom never fixed this recipe for him since he was allergic to peas. She would make it for us kids whenever we were feeling under the weather. This simple and comforting recipe is passed down from my grandmother, to my mother, and now to you.

— *2 tablespoons butter*
— *2 tablespoons flour*
— *2 cups milk*
— *1 can peas (drained)*
— *Bread, sliced and toasted (sourdough, ciabatta, and Italian work well)*

1. Melt butter in pot on the stove. Add flour, stirring constantly.
2. When the mixture is bubbly, gradually add milk. While stirring, bring it to a boil.
3. Reduce heat and simmer for about 2 minutes. Add peas.
4. Toast bread and then put 1 or 2 pieces on each plate.
5. Ladle creamed peas onto the toast and serve.

My Unhealthy Infatuation with Elke Sommer

STILL CAN'T THINK of that one movie she appeared in, though I vaguely recall her in *Circus of the Stars*. That must have been where she met Zsa Zsa Gabor, who said Elke hung out in shabby salons and sold sweaters out of the trunk of her car. She slapped Zsa Zsa with a defamation suit and won.

On YouTube, you can watch Elke's 1994 interview by typing, "Skip E. Lowe Looks at Hollywood." She's sitting on her couch, wearing a floppy hat. She keeps touching it like she's afraid it might disappear.

Skip, the cable host, looks like the poet Mary Oliver if she had been a gnome and taken care to comb her hair. He's perched on a pillow, a hungry bird, constantly chortling and interrupting her as he flies from one question to the next. When Elke says she's fluent in seven languages, he *oohs* and moves on.

A few years after Elke's interview, Skip publishes his autobiography, *The Boy with the Betty Grable Legs*. Tad on Amazon gives it one star. *The New York Times Magazine* profiles Skip with the headline, "Ineptness Has Its Virtues."

Which reminds me, this morning, while waiting for the sluggish banker with sinus problems to review my father's death certificate, I brought up Elke with my mother. *I think she's dead, dear.* When the banker excused herself for the fourth time, my mother rolled her eyes. *So inept,* she whispered, *but so lovely, a dear really.* Then she said, *You are going to write a poem about this, aren't you?*

No, I laughed, thinking the world doesn't need another poem about women who wait while staplers break, their banker returning, followed by two trembling tellers—one carrying a rather large bucket—as the banker warns, *Whatever you do, don't look down.*

Of course, we looked down. And if I could stop thinking about Elke long enough, I'd focus on the middle of the story, before the tellers trap the mouse but not long after my mother—not a fast nor patient woman—scurries outside and chooses to wait in the rain.

*

Though it's not raining in these wedding, village, and beach scenes, Elke has placed umbrellas in the hands of children. Grown-ups too. Even her yellow-haired trees resemble umbrellas. My favorite Elke Sommer's painting is a family of blue figures, their backs to the viewer and their heads obscured by blue umbrellas. Other than a farmhouse in the distance, it's not clear what else they can see. The horizon is a mystery.

On the Official Website of Elke Sommer, you can view some of her artwork. Her acrylic paintings convey an appealing folksy feel. I wish the website featured the blue umbrellas painting as I'd probably buy a lithograph. She's the kind of artist who is not afraid to draw hands and feet. Or umbrellas.

Thank God for YouTube. There's Elke painting. I must have seen "Painting with Elke Sommer" at some point when it ran on PBS. How else did I know she was a painter? Why else would this seem so familiar? At the start of the show, Elke wanders through her garden, smells and plucks a lemon from her tree, and places an arrangement of cut flowers on the coffee table. In fact, the table sits in front of the same brown couch she sat on when she was interviewed by Skip E. Lowe.

You look so simple. Are you simple, Elke?

Complicated but simple, she says.

Biggest lesson you've learned?

Not to trust people.

Oooh, I like that.

I would rather be known as a painter who acts than an actress who paints, Elke has repeatedly said in non-Skip E. Lowe interviews over the years. *It's the only place where I'm not produced, not directed ...*

If I were interviewing Elke, I'd explore her fascination with umbrellas. An umbrella shields, so what was she trying to protect herself from during the 1970s and 1980s? We'd work together to uncover the core meaning of this umbrella symbolism, discussing how, doused in the sorrow of her failed second marriage and three miscarriages, she had turned to umbrellas. I'd point out the stretch where she abandons umbrellas but resurrects them in later work, such as one titled "No Words." Sitting together on her brown couch, we'd study the painting of a man with his back to the viewer. He stands on a stretch of empty highway under a lightning-streaked sky with no shelter in sight from the storm, save for one tiny umbrella blooming on a road sign.

While staring at the painting, it occurs to me that I use Elke like an umbrella. My interest in this Bavarian beauty ebbs and flows. Much like an umbrella, I only pull her out in stormy weather.

*

By the time we reach the next bank, the rain has stopped. For the third time this week, we're escorted to a banker's office. Once again, we're waiting, though the atmosphere in this bank is calm and reassuring. Nobody runs around chasing mice. The manager steps out of the room to make a copy of my father's death certificate.

I point to a painting on the wall. *Cool painting, huh?* I point again. *Mom? See?*

I heard you the first time. I just don't care for it.

Really? But don't you love the colors? The purple trees are so appealing. I like how they drip into the lime-green of the sky.

There are no people in it. I've got to have people in it.

*

In 1980, as part of a Western Michigan University advisory committee for one of his doctoral students, my father went to Libya to help address the public health issue of schistosomiasis, a parasitic disease spread by freshwater snails. Shortly after returning to our home on Creston Street—much like he did after family reunions and taking us on day trips to the Kellogg Biological Station, the Kellogg Bird Sanctuary, and the Kalamazoo Nature Center—my father set his Kodak carousel slide projector on a TV tray and carefully inserted his slides into the rotating machine.

174

Would anybody like to see some pictures? he'd announce, and my brother, sister, and I would scramble into the family room and sprawl on the orange shag carpet. My mother's reply was always the same. *Only if they have people in them.*

As the slide projector hummed and specks of dust danced in the spotlight, pictures, one by one, materialized on the wall. Over the years, each passing image—snow owl, algae dangling from a wooden oar, close-up of ash tree bark, and snails sifted from a Libyan spring—seeped inside me, nourishing my sense of place. Rooted in the grove of the five of us, it was thrilling to find myself entwined with this stunning and messy world. Not even my mother's shouts could unbraid this feeling.

Joe, enough with the trees. Who cares about the water? I don't care about some ancient ruin. Where are the people? Show me the people! Occasionally, when people wandered into his photographs—posing by a pond, leaning into the river, or squinting at the camera—she'd say, *That's more like it!*

*

That was quick, my mother says appreciatively.

The banker smiles. *That's because everything looks in order. And here's the printout of the account activities you requested.* She hands it to my mother and then turns to me. *You are the executor, I assume?*

No, my mother replies. *That would be her sister. Her name is Holly, just like you. And she is excellent with this kind of thing, but she's very busy. So, Jennifer is here instead even though this isn't her forte. She's the poet in the family.*

The banker looks like she wants to say something as she opens and then closes her mouth.

My mother rises. *Holly, I can't thank you enough.* She then points the tip of her cane at me, swishes it to the door, back to me, and then back to the door. I take her cue and head out into the hallway with my mother close behind.

A parade of two, we make our way through the lobby. My mother waves to the tellers, calling them by name. She thanks them with a lightness in her voice that I haven't heard for months. With one hand on her cane and the other grasping my arm, we cross the parking lot as arrows of Canada geese slice south through the autumn skies.

When we reach the car, she says, *While your father may not have been a very trusting person, I am glad he spread things out. You shouldn't put all your eggs in one basket.*

*

Geese wander in and out of many of Elke's paintings. Sometimes, they deposit eggs. In one, a girl strokes a white cat. Having chased geese away moments earlier, the cat rests between two eggs. One is red while the other one is yellow with black polka dots, matching the girl's hat.

A male goose is a gander. When a family of geese gather on the ground, they are also referred to as a gander, but in flight they are called something else. The name escapes me. I'm not thinking of the word *flock* or *gaggle*. My father would know. He knew the names of everything related to the animal world, both spined and spineless. But then he flew away, taking the names with him.

*

In the transfusion room, the last platelets slip down the tubing and into my father's arm. As he rests on the hospital bed, empty blood and platelet bags hang from a silver pole like deflated lungs.

When diagnosed with myelodysplastic syndrome (MDS) a decade ago, doctors referred to it as "a smoldering leukemia," as one out of three diagnosed with the disease progress to acute myeloid leukemia. A normal person's white blood count is four thousand to eleven thousand. In the cavities of my father's bones, his marrow fails him, gushing out sixty thousand to a hundred thousand white blood cells and drowning out any chance for healthy cells to grow. He knows the transfusions aren't prolonging his life. He has only agreed to them in hopes of staying alive long enough for his son to round up his wife and three children and fly into Kalamazoo next week.

All done! the nurse says, bustling about the room and removing the tubes connected to his arm. She slaps her hands above her head. *Sorry about that. I think it's a gnat.* She swats at the air.

I thought it was a mosquito, I say, walking over to the bed as my father slowly swings his legs over the side of the bed. I slip shoes on his feet; this is the first time he has allowed me to help in this way.

I think it's a fly, my mother says.

Maybe a fruit fly? the nurse says. *Though isn't that the same thing as a gnat?*

My husband is an invertebrate zoologist. If anyone would know, he would.

Well, what is it Joe? the nurse asks. *You can't hold out on us like this.*

He doesn't bother to look behind him, where the nurse has resumed with swatting at the air. Exhausted from sitting up, it seems doubtful he's been paying attention to our chatter. Even if he wanted to join in, his gums, swollen and bloody as a result of his low platelets and MDS, make it uncomfortable to talk.

Fly. He says it so softly that both the nurse and my mother, who are on the other side of the bed, ask him to repeat himself.

Fly, I repeat.

Yes, he says. *Let's go with fly.* His shoulders bob up and down, a telltale sign he finds this funny. I start laughing. As my father's shoulders continue to shake, my mother starts giggling. Only the nurse doesn't join in. Her somber expression is a reminder that she is privy to only the last six weeks of this story, the part where sadness seeps in, as evidenced by her patient's rusty smile.

Unlike us, the nurse was never schooled in bugs by my father, never heard him say that you know a fly is a true fly if it has two wings or that it's considered part of the order *Diptera*. *Di* in Greek, of course, means two. Dragonflies, he'd point out, aren't true flies, since they have four wings and thus belong to the order *Odonata,* which means toothed one, referring to their impressively strong, toothed jaw. A dragonfly isn't just a dragonfly. It's a Blue Dasher, a Dragonhunter, an Eastern Pondhawk, and a Widow Skimmer.

The nurse is unable to appreciate her patient's lack of precision in this moment, his willingness to settle for generality and forego a lengthy explanation of flies and their compound eyes. I feel bad that she isn't in on the joke, but clueing her in will only break up this brief party.

While witness to his steady and rapid decline, it is only now, in his permitting the word *fly* to suffice, I realize fully, for the first time, that he is dying. Still, in this knowing, I laugh hard and true, along with my mother, who is also stunned by and swept up in my father's joy.

I wish the others were here with us—my brother and sister, our families, and all those other missing guests who would recognize my father going with *fly* as shorthand for: *I'm releasing a part of who I've been, so I can get on with the business of dying.*

We toast him with laughter, celebrating his life and the creatures he has marveled at, brought to our attention, and named for us.

*

Though they must have delighted me before the age of nine, this is the first dragonfly memory I clearly recall. We're in Big Rapids, Michigan, visiting my grandfather at his cottage on Clear Lake. In a rowboat, my father and I fish for trout and bass. Soon, the rocking motion will lull me to sleep. But before I curl up on the floor of the boat, we'll eat the peanut butter and honey sandwiches he has made for us. Sometime between eating the sandwich and my mother yelling at my father for his failure to apply sunscreen to my burned face, a dragonfly lands on the handle of an oar.

A green darner, my father says. *A male.* He points out the coloring of the dark green thorax, the neon blue of his body. We study the intricate veining of translucent wings that resemble miniature church windows. It's startling to consider the landscape I thought I knew—my grandfather's cottage, the shoreline, the lake, and the boat. Through the wings of a dragonfly, everything feels mysterious, new, and somehow old. Too soon, the green darner flies away, taking his world with him.

*

Shortly before my father died, Representative Sarah Lightner introduced House Bill 4817 to designate the green darner dragonfly as the official insect of Michigan. Since his death, I've been tracking Bill 4817 to see if and when it becomes law.

The insect is named such for resembling a darning needle. A few years ago, when the teeth of an escalator chewed a hole in my brand new maxi dress, my father offered to darn it, a skill he picked up in his army days.

I just now pull the dress out of the closet and search for the tear. It takes several minutes to find. I press my index finger to the area, think of routes traveled, and wonder where we would be were it not for those who came before us.

My father's people migrated to America from Bavaria. My great-grandfather Peter was born in 1853 in Offendorf, Eichstätt, not far from the village of Marloffstein where Elke grew up. It wouldn't surprise me if our ancestors, a mere one hundred and seventeen kilometers from each other, darned in their day. Darning is the lost art of reclaiming what was and pulling together the worn and torn to make new. There exist, however, holes too gaping to close with a needle and thread.

*

180

Crap. Someone else has put forth a bill to designate the monarch as Michigan's state insect. I was about to go outside and rake layers of wet leaves off the lawn. Instead, I compose this letter:

Dear Representative Lightner,

I just wanted to thank you for putting forth House Bill 4817 to designate the green darner dragonfly as the official insect of Michigan. These insects literally fly over the radar of most Michiganders as well as the rest of America. If only folks could have been raised by my father, Joseph Engemann, they too would know that this dragonfly would make a wonderful representation for our state. An invertebrate zoologist born and raised in Belding, Michigan, my father introduced me to the amazing world of these beautiful insects. As I'm sure you know, there is exciting research emerging on these most excellent flyers who journey great distances to reach us each year. Annually, it takes three generations to travel their migratory loop, following the same paths their great greats took.

I read that another bill has recently been introduced to designate the monarch butterfly as our state insect. Of course, who doesn't love a monarch? However, it feels more Michigan to me to select the less flashy, hard-working insect who more easily eludes our attention. While the monarch is sipping nectar from a flower, the green darner is busy feasting on Michigan pests like mosquitoes.

If my math is correct, twenty-two of our forty-eight states that have designated a state insect have selected butterflies, seven of them are the monarch. Yawn! Michigan is more original than that, and I would hope our state insect would convey this message. With more than seven hundred Michigan insects to choose from, I'm glad you put forth the green darner.

I'll keep tracking your bill to see if and when it becomes law.

Crossing my fingers,
Jennifer Clark

I email the letter to Sarah Lightner, hoping it might buoy her spirits and provide further support for the green darner.

*

Lately, Elke's been keeping a low profile. Recent images suggest she is hanging out in Germany with her third husband. The only negative thing you can say about her is that she has a penchant for ugly hats.

I should figure out what to fix for dinner. Instead, I scroll through online images of Elke at the 2014 Octoberfest in Munich, Germany. At least she's not wearing a hat, though I'm not keen on the floral wreath adorning her head. She's wearing the traditional Octoberfest outfit, a white blouse under a tight-fitting Bavarian dirndl. The long dress is a striking green; the color reminds me of a darner. My gaze drifts to the window overlooking the backyard. The grass is smothered in yellow leaves. Deer wander in and out of the frame. Elke says, *Each painting tells a story.* What is the story here? If she were with me right now, I'd tell her, *Deer in brown coats are made for fall.*

The phone rings. I don't feel like answering it.

Elke says, *You should put a nice frame around your finished work.* How do you know when your work is finished? Is it ever?

The day before my father died, he said he had one more post he wanted to write and upload to his blog, *Evolution Insights*. For six years, he'd been sharing his thinking about evolution, science, creativity, and God with the world. He never got to write that final post.

The phone is still ringing. I pick it up. It's my brother, John, calling on his way home from work. He sounds happy. *I made Kung Pao Chicken for dinner last night. Best Kung Pao recipe I've ever made. The kids and Ashley loved it. I'll send you the recipe if you want. Not sure what we'll have for supper tonight. What are you doing?*

I should be cooking dinner, tackling laundry, and writing thank you cards. *I'm thinking about Elke Sommer.*

Didn't she used to be on The Mike Douglas Show?

After supper—thank God for Trader Joe's Beef and Broccoli—I check into that possibility. It looks like Mike's talk show ran from 1961 to 1982 and enjoyed wide syndication. He regularly had cohosts like Redd Foxx, Soupy Sales, Richard Pryor, and even John Lennon and Yoko Ono. Oh, and Ethel Merman. I bet she sang "There's No Business Like Show Business." Wait. Ethel and her spectacularly thin eyebrows were on the show but only as a guest.

Bingo! Elke cohosted for a week in 1973. My brother would have been a wee one, so he must have seen the show when it went into syndication. Up until 1965, the show aired live five days a week. That changed once Elke's nemesis, Zsa Zsa, appeared as a guest. Perturbed when another guest, Morey Amsterdam, interrupted her, Zsa Zsa called him a son of a bitch. After that, the show switched to taping.

I can't stop searching for Elke. She appeared on *The Gong Show*, *Hollywood Squares*, *The Muppet Show*, and several Bob Hope specials, including one taped in 1967 on the campus of University of California, Los Angeles. O.J. Simpson was also one of Bob's guests. That brings to mind a connection between Elke and O.J. Judge Lance Ito, who presided over O.J.'s murder trial in which he was acquitted, also presided over Elke's defamation suit, and Zsa Zsa was ordered to pay millions.

*

After we grew up and moved out of my parents' house, they got a dog, a Lhasa Apso. She came named: Ellke. The breed boasts a pleasing temperament, one that is friendly, enchanting, and playful. Ellke was none of these. Loving and loyal only to my parents, she harbored viciousness in her ten-inch stature. The American Kennel Association tactfully notes that some can be "charry with strangers." She was charry as hell. During a Thanksgiving visit, while in the middle of passing a green bean casserole to my sister sitting next to me, Ellke bit my ankle and drew blood.

You must have looked at her, my father said, gently patting Ellke's head as she snarled at me.

*

The day after his last transfusion and a week before he died, I drove out to Norman Camera and bought a slide converter. Over the next several days, I converted a handful of slides to digital images, just a fraction of the ones he had neatly labeled and stored in dozens of mismatched cases. In front of his chair, I set up a TV tray with my laptop. I angled the screen, so he could see what he had seen: his father ice fishing on Slayton Lake, his army buddies crossing a stream in Munich, his sister Jane and her boy canoeing the Pinnebog, his young bride standing beside a peach tree, his son at five waving a miniature American flag in front of his blue Ford station wagon, my toes as they appeared in 1981, a closeup of Holly's mouth and braces from that same year, and a hummingbird's nest he discovered in the fork of a branch ...

A hummingbird's nest is built for change. It's the female who builds the cup-shaped nest, weaving spider silk amongst bits of leaves and lichen, moss and plants. Her construction cradles eggs the size of a navy bean and then expands as hatchlings grow. Most of us don't even notice these thumb-sized nests. Looking up, it appears to be a bump on a branch. Looking down, one sees only an umbrella of leaves.

My mother navigates the array of items collected over the years. She wonders aloud why her mate collected stamps, coins, and shells, padding their nest with cufflinks he never wore and bill statements he paid decades ago. *I just don't understand your father. I only wish I could get into his brain and figure out what he saw in all this junk.* Recycling memory after memory, she cleans out the nest.

propping open door
husband's brown shoe welcomes her
a lost wing, waiting

Hummingbirds and humans share the same gene for singing and vocalization. The language of grief hovers and hums. Some days, we fly backwards.

*

I wonder where Elke is right now. Wherever she is, I hope she's still painting.

*

Several weeks after the funeral, I show my mother the 115th photo converted from slide.

Your father took that?

Yes. According to his slide, he labeled it "Fall Colors at Gold Lake, 1953."

I hold my breath, waiting for her to yell. There are no people in it. Instead, my father has captured this Michigan lake, its clear face wearing sky splattered in burnt umber, orange ochre, cinnamon, and crimson.

She is silent but then, *Fall was always his favorite season.* Holding the lake in her hands, she takes a deep breath, dives in, and for a moment, sees what he saw. *Beautiful,* she says. *Just beautiful.*

Best Kung Pao Chicken Recipe Ever

Serves 4

My brother has made many Kung Pao Chicken meals and says, *Ten years ago, I would have suggested a more complex, authentic recipe, but this one from Cook's Country turns out great. It's easy, and you get great results.*

— *1 ½ pounds chicken, cubed*
— *1 cup chicken broth, low-sodium*
— *3 tablespoons oyster sauce*
— *2 teaspoons hot sauce*
— *2 teaspoons corn starch*
— *3 tablespoons vegetable oil*
— *½ cup dry-roasted peanuts*
— *1 red bell pepper, cut in ½ inch pieces*
— *3 garlic cloves, minced*
— *1 tablespoon fresh ginger, grated*
— *Rice*
— *Broccoli*

1. Whisk together the broth, oyster sauce, corn starch, and hot sauce. (My brother uses Sriracha but says a hot sauce like Cholula would work just as well.) Set aside.

2. In a nonstick skillet, heat 2 tablespoons of the oil over medium-high heat. Just as it begins to smoke, add the chicken and peanuts.

3. Cook for about 4 minutes or until the chicken is browned. Empty contents into a bowl so you can use the same skillet.

4. Add the rest of the oil to the empty skillet, and as it begins to smoke, add the pepper.

5. Cook for 3 minutes and then toss in the garlic and ginger.

6. Add the broth mixture and bring to a boil.

7. Return the chicken and peanuts to the skillet and simmer everything until the sauce thickens and the chicken is thoroughly cooked.

8. Serve with rice and steamed broccoli.

Extraordinarily unordinary times cry out for the desperately ordinary

SINCE THE PANDEMIC hit, my sister can't stop making soap. Or talking about it.

We're on her back deck, six feet apart, sipping strawberry jalapeño margaritas.

This soap thing rocks! she says. And she's rocked quite a few soaps, from Sassy Citrus to Date Night to Grandma's Lemon Bars, turning out loaf after beautiful loaf.

To make her soaps, Holly buys refined shea butter, rice bran oil, essential oils, and pounds of sodium hydroxide, all delivered safely through the mail. She obtains avocado, castor, and hemp oils from a local health food store. For some batches, she snatches eggs, still warm from her hens, and adds them in. Into others, she drizzles milk from coconuts or goats.

Three months into the pandemic, she placed a custom order with some guy named Jeremy for a soap cutter made from solid cherry. She drove seventy-six miles to pick it up. She now slices Strawberry and Lemon Poppy Seed loaves with ease. With wild abandon, she gives away Cucumber Melon and Sexy Beast Mowing the Lawn.

She drives across town delivering soap to relatives, former coworkers, soccer moms, and book-club friends she sees now only on Zoom. To the Amazon delivery person, she gives

Sideways Smile Sandalwood. The other day she slipped some fresh slabs to the masked salesladies at J.Jill. She's hauled an assortment to the grocery store and let these essential workers choose the bars that spoke to them. Even before these recipients use the soap, I imagine they feel, like me, already lathered in her love.

Hol, that was so cool how you wove that twine around that almond soap you gave me. You should do that with all your soaps.

I don't want to get distracted by packaging. It's what's inside that matters. Holly goes on about the essential oils she wants to infuse into her next batch. She talks so fast that I can't follow. Instead, I marvel how the sun has found its way through the trees and is kissing her face. She shines.

In times of fear and anxiety, some people flounder while others, like my sister, unfold and open themselves anew. She's now your gal for sunburn, poison ivy, eczema, and psoriasis. In this age of uncertainty, in which the world's economy has shrunk along with our lives, she offers plenty of options. Need a vacation? She'll gift you one. *Little vacation soaps*, she calls them. Made with chamomile and honey. Scrub the tiny rosebud over your body. Breathe deeply. For a more rustic getaway, try her Pine Tar, a bar that *smells like a smoky, closed-up cabin.*

Itching to host a big party with guests close and touching, shoulders bumping? Slather yourself in Confetti. Missing the bar scene? Suds up with some Coconut Porter. If you're craving something more spiritual and happen to be walking down a street in Kalamazoo, Amazing Grace, humming with lemon and jasmine, may arrive to you unbidden and unmerited.

In response to her soap gifts, Holly has received face masks, a four-pack of Founders ale, blueberry buckle, wines, peach jam, sour-cherry jam, tart-cherry jam, an infinity scarf, chocolate chip cookies, hand-knitted soap savers, homemade Bloody Mary mix, and sourdough bread.

You need to sell your soaps, I say, sipping my margarita. *Put up a website. Start making some money. And you're going to have to change some of the soap names. Mouse Poop Lavender isn't enticing. Who wants to rub that on—*

It smells delish!

And Big Ass Orange Addict—

People love that one! she says, laughing. *It's got notes of tobacco and vanilla. Half the fun is coming up with the names, so I'm not changing them. Anyways, I can't sell my soap. It would suck the joy right out of it.*

I ask what else she's gotten lately.

Gratitude and love, she says. *That's all I need.*

Fueled by an economy of kindness, she labors deep into the heat of summer. During these extraordinarily unordinary times, her desperately ordinary work brings joy to both the giver and the receiver.

In this time when we physically distance and avoid touching even our own faces, Holly has figured out how to embrace weary spirits residing inside flesh. Each nourishing soap, whether bartered or given away, restores hope and serves as a reminder that, beneath the grime of despair, we are part of the slathery goodness thrumming wildly in this world.

Not a day slips by that Holly isn't texting photos of her latest creation, each loaf a canvas of comfort waiting to be shared. I hope these soap interruptions are welcome diversions for our brother, John. As an infectious disease doctor and hospital epidemiologist, he is extremely busy these days.

Forty-six batches of soap later, our brother texts back: *Dear Tiny Baby Jesus, Please allow me to have at least one-tenth of the joy that soapmaking gives Holly in all that I do each day. Amen.*

Amen, brother.

Strawberry Jalapeño Margaritas

Yields 2

This is Holly's own recipe. Warning: It may be difficult to follow.

— *6 glugs of tequila*
— *Jalapenos*
— *3 glugs of Triple Sec*
— *1 glop of frozen strawberries*
— *Nellie's Key West Lime Juice*
— *Drop of honey (optional)*
— *Sea salt*

1. Gather a blender and the above supplies. You don't want to be hunting down ingredients while making this luscious beverage. I recommend the tequila with the Day of the Dead skeleton head on the bottle as it is great with heat. If you don't have this on hand, Costco tequila will suffice. This recipe assumes you have previously bought too many jalapeños and sliced them to fit into the tequila bottle to macerate until they turn a lovely shade of 70's jade green. (Wait one day minimum to release their goodness. One week for superb.)

2. Plop a handful of strawberries into the blender. For each handful, add a glug, glug, glug, glug, glug, glug of tequila, a dainty half (three glugs) of Triple Sec, and three quick whizzes of lime. If the strawberries aren't super sweet, add a drop of honey. If you're not going to fancy the edge of your margarita glasses with salt, add 1 ½ grinds of sea salt. Add an additional jalapeño, sliced, if desired. (Remove seeds as they aren't pleasant to sip.)

3. Blitz the goodness out of everything just until the strawberry is puréed.

4. Pour over ice in fancy glasses and enjoy.

You may substitute mango, watermelon, or peaches for the strawberries.

Acknowledgments & Notes

I'm grateful to the editors of the publications in which the following pieces first appeared:

The Sonder Review, "A Fleeting History of Phylum, Class, Order, and Family."

Pear Noir! "Apology to the Grayling."

Flyway: Journal of Writing & Environment, "Measured Thoughts on Cooking (in no particular order)." Essay nominated for a Pushcart Prize.

Storm Cellar, "Mango Jesus."

Spittoon, "A Nod to Ernest Borgnine."

You are here: The Journal of Creative Geography at the University of Arizona, "What I Wanted to Say."

Concho River Review, "Kissing the World Goodbye."

Raven Chronicles, "Time Traveling on Creston Street."

Cardinal Sins, "Fourth Grade Place Settings." A later version of this piece (as it appears now) was published in *A Beginner's Guide to Heaven* (Unsolicited Press).

Thank you, Poetry Dawgs, even those of you who grumbled when I brought prose instead of poems to our group. It was worth it. Your critiques always make my work better.

Great appreciation to you, Donna Carroll, for first reading this manuscript and, as usual, offering helpful feedback.

Stacy Nowicki, thank you for encouraging me to add the recipes. The book is much tastier because of you.

I am indebted in so many ways to my brother, John Engemann, and my sister, who refuses to let me use her real name in this book. You are two of the best people and cooks I know. This book would not exist without either of you.

Gratitude to my parents, Joseph and Nancy Engemann, two of the best teachers I've ever had. While working on this book, I didn't realize that my father would soon teach our family his final lesson—how to kiss the world goodbye. He did it brilliantly. Mom, thank you for teaching us how, even in the face of tremendous loss, to say hello to the world.

John and Tom, thank you for bearing with me through butter, Borgnine, and all things in between. I love you both so much.

Some notes on "Butter Love":

My father's blog, *Evolution Insights*, can be found here:
  evolutioninsights.blogspot.com.

The two poems referenced within this piece can be found in
  Surdas: Sur's Ocean, ed. Kenneth E. Bryant and trans.
  John S. Hawley, (Massachusetts: Harvard University
  Press, 2015), poem #7, p. 19 and poem #17, p. 33.

Quotes referencing the Oleomargarine Act were taken from
  U.S. Congress, House, "House Resolution 366" before
  the 71st Congress, *Congressional Record* (February 25,
  1931), pp. 5990-5992.

"Mrs. Roosevelt Does a TV Commercial," Thomas Louis Stix,
  Harper's Magazine, November 1963, pp. 104-106.
  (Quote taken from p. 105.)

A study referenced within this piece is "The Economic
  Impacts of Immigrant Labor on U.S. Dairy Farms,"
  Flynn Adcock, David Anderson, and Parr Rosson.
  Prepared for National Milk Producers Federation, August
  2015.

When Dave the Potter was emancipated in 1864, he took the
  last name "Drake," after a former owner. It is believed he
  died sometime in the 1870s. When Leonard Todd
  learned that his family members had owned the artisan,

Todd wrote *Carolina Clay: The Life and Legend of the Slave Potter, Dave* (W.W. Norton, Fall 2008). Todd also maintains an interesting website at: leonardtodd.com.

Discovering Dave: Spirit Captured in Clay is a documentary produced by filmmaker Mark Albertin of Scrapbook Video Productions and archeologist George Wingard of the Savannah River Archaeological Research program. Wingard has uploaded it to Vimeo, and you can watch it by going here: *vimeo.com/145320466.*

A note on "Extraordinarily unordinary times cry out for the desperately ordinary":

The title of this piece was inspired by the following quote from Proctor & Gamble, makers of Ivory Soap, which made its debut in 1879: *Soap is a desperately ordinary substance to us.*

About the Author

JENNIFER CLARK is the author of three full-length poetry collections: *A Beginner's Guide to Heaven* (Unsolicited Press), *Johnny Appleseed: The Slice & Times of John Chapman,* and *Necessary Clearings* (both published by Shabda Press). She is also the coeditor of the anthology *Immigration & Justice For Our Neighbors* (Celery City Books). She's authored a children's book on college awareness, *What Do You See In Room 21 C?* (Celery City Books), and her poems, essays, and fiction have appeared in numerous literary journals, magazines, and anthologies. She lives in Kalamazoo, Michigan, with her husband John and son Tom. Her website is jenniferclarkkzoo.com.

About the Press

Unsolicited Press was founded in 2012 and is based in Portland, Oregon. The press produces stellar fiction, nonfiction, and poetry from award-winning writers. Authors include John W. Bateman, T.K. Lee, Rosalia Scalia, and Brook Bhagat.

Find the press on Twitter and Instagram: @unsolicitedp

Learn more at www.unsolicitedpress.com.

CPSIA information can be obtained
at www.ICGtesting.com
Printed in the USA
LVHW030021010322
712228LV00004B/240